Seven to Seventy

My Journey through Time

Dear Joyce

LAVERA GOODEYE

Lavera Goodeye

iUniverse LLC
Bloomington

SEVEN TO SEVENTY
MY JOURNEY THROUGH TIME

iUniverse books may be ordered through booksellers or by contacting:

iUniverse
1663 Liberty Drive
Bloomington, IN 47403
www.iuniverse.com
1-800-Authors (1-800-288-4677)

Because of the dynamic nature of the Internet, any web addresses or links contained in this book may have changed since publication and may no longer be valid. The views expressed in this work are solely those of the author and do not necessarily reflect the views of the publisher, and the publisher hereby disclaims any responsibility for them.

Any people depicted in stock imagery provided by Thinkstock are models, and such images are being used for illustrative purposes only. Certain stock imagery © Thinkstock.

ISBN: 978-1-4917-1398-3 (sc)
ISBN: 978-1-4917-1400-3 (hc)
ISBN: 978-1-4917-1399-0 (e)

Library of Congress Control Number: 2013920318

Printed in the United States of America.

iUniverse rev. date: 12/13/2013

"Delta Dawn"
Words and Music by T. Alex Harvey, Larry Collins
United Artists Music Co., Inc./ Big Ax Music/ASCAP
1973 Capital Records, Inc. no copyright infringement intended

"Gladiola"
Words and Music by Alan Gordon
©1976 BMG Platinum Songs (BMI)/R2M Music
All rights administered by BMG Rights Management (US) LLC.
Used by Permission. All Rights Reserved.

"I'm Moving On"
Words and Music by Phillip Brian White
©2000 Bug Music (BMI)/ Murrah Music, Inc.,
All rights administered by BUG Music, Inc., a BMG Chrysalis company.
Used by Permission. All Rights Reserved.

To my two nephews, Munir and Derek

> "Do not be afraid of them, for I am with you to deliver you," says the Lord. Then the Lord put out his hand and touched my mouth: and the Lord said to me, "Now I have put my words in your mouth."
>
> —Jeremiah 1:8–9

Contents

Preface

I watch Dr. Phil because his program deals with mental and emotional issues. I appreciate the value of this program, as people are just beginning to feel comfortable with these topics. I was watching one of his shows, which was about a lovely and intelligent young girl who was bullied by other girls at her school, when I had an insight into how the effects of bullying continue after the events are long over. We punish ourselves with messages of not being good enough. Dr. Phil tells us that we should give ourselves a more positive self-description.

I tend to bully myself because I feel that I'm not strong or smart enough to talk myself out of having the feelings I still have after 70 years. The events of my childhood affected me so deeply that I am now trying to heal from them by writing my story. My mother's suicide, when I was age 6, was more extreme than bullying is. I know that Dr. Phil's program is not the one-hour solution it seems to be, however. Sometimes people have to work with counsellors to continue their healing.

I have consulted mental health workers while on my journey to wholeness. At one time, the only things I read were self-help books that included stories of people dealing with problems similar to mine. I also attended workshops and support groups, as well as college and university programs and classes, to learn how to help myself and others.

My heart goes out to people who are beating themselves up for not achieving their dreams and for not overcoming oppression and depression. It is easier for me to cry and identify with the plights of others than to have compassion for myself on my own journey. I am the oldest among my siblings. I thought that my purpose was to help others and do what they needed. I didn't think that I deserved to be loved and appreciated. I hope now to care for myself and break through to feel the joy of being.

One of my struggles is with the judgmental teachings of evangelical religion to which I was subjected. My goal is to speak my truth and have it mean something in the lives of others. My conflict is with a society that doesn't want to hear me. I try to value myself and be valued. I try to get past the hurt that has come into my life. Others try to convince me to turn the bad into good. Some want to hear only happy stories. It would be nice if someone held and comforted me while I cried.

My journey to healing has shown me that Canada's Native people have experienced shame and been stigmatized and that sometimes they commit suicide. I was drawn to them, and they subsequently played a role in restoring my confidence. Most of my life, I struggled to be accepted, to feel like part of a community and to come home to my own spiritual safe place.

People who have achieved great success seem to be honoured on television. If someone who acts in movies or who plays professional sports writes a book, then that book is reviewed and sells thousands of copies. The writers appear on talk shows, where the studio audience is given copies of their books. I know I will have a more difficult time reaching my audience.

Throughout the winter of 2012–13, I sat at my desk in front of my south-facing window and brought together my previous writings to compose this memoir page by page. Some of my recollections were sad, and as a result I felt the strong feelings I had expected. The people of Coronation complained bitterly about our winter. This seemed to be the only topic of conversation. The winter was longer than ever and brought more storms and more snow than we had seen in a long time. Not for one moment did I think to complain about the weather. Snow needed shovelling; I could get my exercise and stay physically fit while doing it.

I have experienced depression during other winters, but the act of writing my story buoyed me throughout this one. I've enjoyed the process. I found my publisher, iUniverse, and enjoyed the support of the consultants Traci Anderson and Kathi Wittkamper.

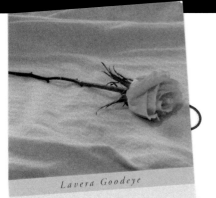

Grandparents Establish Family on the Prairie

As I move into this new millennium, I have reflected throughout my life. I choose to begin when my grandparents came to Alberta more than a hundred years ago. Both of my parents and my stepmother were born and lived all their lives in this rural area, which was officially established when the railroad first brought its trains through in 1910 and 1911.

The towns were established as the railroad track moved east from the larger centres. When I was growing up, all of these prairie towns featured grain elevators, wherein the grain was stored until it was transported either east or west by train. Then at that point, the grain would be put on a boat, shipped and eventually sold around the world. My hometown boasted three such elevators.

Coronation has been described as a place where the parkland meets the prairie. To the north of the town, there are groves of aspen trees and some spruce along the river valley. The south is more open. Antelope appreciate the prairie, and deer like to hide in the trees. Both can be seen enjoying our landscape.

The groves of poplars are dying because their lifespan isn't as long as mine. Survey crews easily mapped out this land into 160-acre quarter sections and 640-acre sections. (A section is one square mile.) Road allowances run north and south every mile, and east and west every two miles. Sometimes a road was built, but if it hadn't been, then the farmer fenced the land and used it until a road was needed.

A feature of my homeland is the Nose Hills to the east. When we children stepped up the stairs in our grandfather's house, we could look out the east-facing window and see the hills' variegated blue line on the horizon. The Nose Hills create an incline that rises to the south and drops off suddenly in a nose. Our Native people named these hills. As a tool for navigating they visualized a man lying on his back and stretching across Alberta. The Hand Hills were farther south and west, and then came the Knee Hills and Foothills.

The Nose Hills are part of the Neutral Hills. Native legend says that the Great Spirit caused these hills to rise up during a longstanding war wherein many braves died. The Cree and Blackfoot eventually buried their hatchets and made peace.

A local history book compiled in 1967, *Shadows of the Neutrals,* discusses the significance of Native people to this area. It includes the legend of the Great Spirit creating the Neutral Hills. It also includes the contribution of the missionaries, who worked extensively with First Nations inhabitants of the area to help them accommodate the oncoming rush of settlers.

Reverend John McDougall retired in the year that Grampa came to Fleet. My father was born on the day Father Lacombe died. The Catholic priest and the Methodist missionary spent their last days within 10 miles of each other. Both passed away within a month of each other.

My grandfather Sam Annett from Northern Ireland claimed his homestead in 1905. He established our family farm almost a mile south of the location where the town of Fleet would later be created.

Fleet hasn't grown very much over the years. When I was still going to school, we counted all the people living in the hamlet. There were 104. I used to say that the town was called Fleet because people seemed to be fleeting away. The community hall is still available for social functions. Homes remain, but none of the stores or schools operate anymore. The church where my sister and I married our husbands stands proud and empty. I wouldn't be able to find our skating rink. Trees now fill that area.

When the land is flat and empty, the naming of towns is difficult. Two towns in Alberta were named for their physical features: Two Hills and Three Hills. Saskatchewan was similarly void of unique features, so towns were given names like Superb, Success or Major, indicating hopefulness for a bright future.

Canadian Pacific Railroad honoured our line of towns by relating them and their people to English royalty. Driving east from Fleet, one finds the towns of Federal, Coronation, Throne, Veteran, Loyalist, Consort and Monitor.

In Coronation, I can stop my 2006 Toyota Yaris at the corner of Victoria and Albert and contemplate my family's beginnings on this prairie before Fleet was given a name.

My mother's father, Joseph Wideman, and his brother, Wilmot, arrived in this prairie area in 1906. My mother's Mennonite family was quick to build their Markham Community Church three or four miles north of our farm after they had settled.

A large group of Pennsylvania Dutch Mennonites had left Markham, Ontario, to set up farming communities in Alberta. Many settled amidst the rich farming land of Didsbury and Carstairs. When they had run out of room in that part of Alberta, the two Wideman brothers were among the settlers who came to Fleet where the soil is less productive.

Henry and Elizebeth Wideman left Pennsylvania and cleared the homestead in Ontario. They built the cut-stone house that I saw and photographed in 1973. By that time, it was at the edge of Metropolitan Toronto.

Henry and Elizebeth had four sons and five daughters. Their seventh child, Martin, was the one who inherited the family home. Joseph and Wilmot were his two oldest children. There were five younger children, as well. The youngest son, Wesley, would come to live in the stone house. When we were children, Wesley and his wife, Agnes, were our visitors. He would have been in his fifties at the time—and he was handsome and robust.

When Ira and Roxie Weeks and their family came to their homestead in 1906, at a place called Lindsville, the train brought them as far as Lacombe. The entire family travelled for three days from Tillsonburg, Ontario, in boxcars that also held their household effects and farm animals. They had to arrange wagons for their oxen to take them the rest of the way to their new home near the Battle River.

Pearl, grandmother to my three half-brothers, was already 6 years old when she came to Alberta with her family. The Weeks children who arrived from Ontario were Clara, Pearl, Ross and Elsie. I think that George, Hazel and Omar were born in Alberta. Their mother died after Omar was born. It was Ross who established his Weeks family beside my relatives in the Markham community of Alberta.

Milton Strome married Pearl Weeks and established his family at Beaverdale. My grandfather Joseph Wideman and Mike Troyer travelled there to minister to Strome's family and encourage their attendance at Markham's vacation Bible school—or camp meeting—and at church services. I think that my mother's parents took their straw ticks to use as mattresses when they connected with the people at the camp meeting in Didsbury.

My grandmother Ellen Beck came to Stettler by train. She arrived on April 22, 1909. Grampa told me the story of walking to Stettler and discovering by letter or telegraph that his wife was arriving on the train that day. He had to walk back to his homestead to get his horses. My grandparents were married that day in Stettler, and

Grampa drove Gramma home with a horse and wagon, not the carriage I had envisioned. He brought her to live in a two-room shack that later served as a granary. It stood in the barnyard next to our well and water trough for many years.

Sam and Ellen grew up in Kilkeel, in County Down, a rural community in Northern Ireland, and they had known each other before Grampa came to work in silver mines in the States and Mexico. When he sent word that he had a homestead in Alberta, she was already working as a seamstress and staying with Grampa's brother's family in New York City.

Grampa told stories from his homeland of Ireland— stories of fairies, witches and ghosts. One of these begins with him as a young boy walking down the road.

An old woman said to him, "There will be a death in that house."

Grampa asked, "How do you know?"

She said, "I can see a coffin going in the chimney."

Grampa was not convinced.

She said, "You can't see it? Here, take my hand."

When he took her hand, he saw the coffin.

Most of the magic stayed behind in Ireland, but it happened on more than one occasion that a rooster came up to the door of the house and crowed. This was seen as an omen. Word would come all the way from Ireland that there was a death in the family.

Grampa was against the papists, as he called them, but his life in Canada exhibited none of the strife that still troubles his homeland. I often heard Grampa talk about purgatory, usually in a joking way. I found it to be a lovely, long and interesting word. I thought it was a place that Catholics reserved for Protestants. Right now, my chime clock is in purgatory while the repairman enjoys his winter in Arizona.

Much later in my life, I found out that our Annett name is really of French origin. One of my relatives reported that our family consisted of Protestant Huguenots who had left Catholic France to go to Scotland. They got as far as Northern Ireland and settled at Kilkeel beside the Irish Sea.

In Ireland there is a guesthouse called Sam's Cottage on land that was intended to be my grandfather's inheritance. When he saw the 17-acre plot, which included a view of the hill and home where my grandmother lived, he knew he wanted more for himself and the woman he hoped to marry. He packed his bags and left for America.

Gramma had two daughters, Helene and Minnie, in 1913, when the train brought her two sisters. Martha Beck married Gordon Booth. They settled a mile east and had a daughter, Muriel. Lydia married Howard Saunders on a farmstead one mile west. The couple had one daughter, Ethel, and two sons, Howard Jr. and Gordon.

That year the Slemp family, which included 11 of their 12 children, moved from the southern United States to a farm near the Booths'. Earl and Leo married two of Gordon Booth's sisters, so my father had Muriel as a cousin in common with the Slemps.

My grandfather built the two-storey farmhouse. The two girls were older than my father, whose name was John, and older than the twins, Willie and Doreen, who were born after my father was. When I was in junior high at Fleet, I found an old school register. My father and the twins were in the same high school grade. When I asked my father about this, he said that the twins had caught up to him.

I am thinking of an old song we loved to sing as kids: "My Grandfather's Clock." We emphasized the line "And it stopped short, never to go again, when the old man died."

The song includes the phrase "90 years without faltering." In the time of our grandfathers, a life of 90 years was an impossible goal. My grandfather's last surviving son died at age 92.

When people of the third generation in Alberta were singing the "Tick, Tock" song, most of us were living with or were close to grandfathers who'd come from somewhere else. Only the Cree, Blackfoot and Métis— and a rare few non-Natives—were born here in Alberta. Most had come from Europe, eastern Canada or the States. These men and their wives had struck out from the past to start a new life in a wild, unknown land. The buffalo had already been wiped out to make room for farming and railroads.

Our grandparents were inspired by the promise of 160 acres of land and opportunity. They came from large families. There was not enough land in Ireland or in Ontario to accommodate the younger generation. Grampa Annett had five older brothers. He also had two older and two younger sisters. The Wideman brothers were the oldest sons of a seventh child. They left Ontario to leave room in the house for their five younger brothers and sisters.

My grandparents and their neighbours held close to their hearts ideas from their homeland and from the people they had left behind. They did everything they could to establish their families. Grampa built the farmhouse and the hip-roof barn, each on its own small knoll. Sheep, draft horses, black cows and clucky hens with broods of fluffy yellow, red and black chicks populated the yard and fields.

The milk was fresh from the cows' udders each morning and night. While the milk was still warm, it was run through the cream separator. Pigs or the pail-bunter calves of the milk-producing cows drank the skim milk. Cream was saved to make butter, or else it was sold in cans to the creamery in Castor. Young girls took turns lifting and lowering the plunger in the crock butter churn. It was hard to stay with the task long enough to hear the splash as the lumps of butter separated from the buttermilk.

Straw was thrown into a hole of winter snow and formed an ice well, which cooled the summer milk and cream to prevent souring. Eggs were cleaned and sold, as well.

Our soon-to-be summer meals picked at grain in the yard. Two or three young fryer chickens would be caught and tied to the clothesline. Young people had to learn how to tie them with binder twine and cut off their heads with a butcher knife. Then they would run away and watch from a distance while the chickens flapped their wings and bled out. The teenagers would cut them down when they were ready to pluck, and then they'd clean and cook them.

After the Fleet School was built in 1920, the Annett children attended classes there. They were able to continue onto high school because the first rural high school in Alberta was built there in 1921. My aunts Helene and Minnie started school together. They must have been among the first students in Fleet School.

Improved yields and favourable grain prices provided the money our family needed to buy telephones and motorcars in the 1920s.

The prosperous years faded into the dry, dusty times of the 1930s, when my parents were beginning their adult lives and finding mates. Hard times had to be endured. The crops dried up and the fields began to blow away. If there was a garden, it provided a cellar full of potatoes and turnips. Corn and peas were dried and stored in syrup cans. Jars of canned berries, jams and pickles were also stored. A heater in the cellar prevented them from freezing. The animals provided meat, eggs and milk.

Minnie helped me visualize the time before I was born, when my parents were getting to know each other. She wrote this:

> Dad and us kids all went to church and Sunday school in Fleet on Sunday mornings. In the afternoon after we had the car (1929), Mom and all of us went to church and Sunday school again at Markham, about four miles north of Fleet. We used to like that, as there were about fifteen young people and we all sat together in the back three or four rows. This class was just for unmarried folks, so we got a kick out of the fact that Artie Troyer used to have to sit with us. He must have been in his late forties. After church, everyone used to stand around and visit for maybe an hour or so. Every Sunday, we either had some family home for supper or went to some home. The meals were fabulous, and we always had two kinds of dessert. Mrs. Spencer's father, Mr. Burkholder, used to travel around the country and sell Bibles and mottoes and religious books.

It seems very clear to me that these young people giggled and flirted, or maybe just looked shy and embarrassed, and found their life partners on those Sundays at Markham. This explains why three Annetts married three Widemans. Some people, my mother among them, went to Mountain View Bible School at Didsbury and had a chance to meet other young people. My father wanted to attend Olds Agricultural School, but he stayed home to farm.

My father left the farm to work for my mother's brother Harvey for a short time during the 1930s when his wage was $4 a month. My father's brother went to Seattle to study for the ministry. He married my mother's cousin, Muriel Wideman. My father's older sister, Helene, was already married to my mother's brother, Allen Wideman, who was also in the ministry. The other twin, Doreen, was sick with kidney disease and died before I went to school.

Artie Troyer later came to help Daddy with work around the farm when we were too young to be of much assistance. One day, my father and Artie were sawing wood with a big round blade saw powered by the belt off the tractor. Dad was nervous because Artie was careless and often put himself in danger of getting hurt by the saw.

Artie would help plant potatoes. Dad would pull the three-bottom plough with the tractor, and Artie would sit on the plow and drop potatoes through a pipe. One blade would open the furrow, and the next one would drop the dirt over the seed potato. For seed, we would cut our own potatoes, which had been stored in the cellar over winter.

My Childhood Home

My mother married my father in 1938. They had three daughters: Lavera, born November 1939; Joan, born October 1940; and Julia, born September 1942.

When I was born, two months after Hitler's invasion of Poland, our home was a little three-room house at the bottom of the hill that held Grampa's house. It was built on the east side of the Manitoba maple trees that surrounded the Annett potato patch and garden. Beside our house, a lane lead from the barnyard north to the east–west road and the field we crossed to get to the town of Fleet.

My mother was taken away to the mental hospital in Ponoka when I was 3, after Julia was born. I have no memory of losing my mother that way. In those days, things weren't explained to children. Your mother disappeared. Our older family members might have hoped that we wouldn't notice.

My mother was in the mental hospital for a year. I'm not sure how much was known at the time about postpartum depression, but I believe that if she had been born in a later generation, then she would have been diagnosed with it. My mother was of German descent. The whole world was involved in the insanity of war. I thought how sensible it was for her to be in a mental hospital.

Over the course of my life, I have searched for information about my ancestors and their lives. As an adult, I am ready to process the events of my childhood. My struggle is to find insight and deal with the conflict and loss I've carried with me all these years.

I had to ask myself which woman was my mother the first time I saw my baby sister, Julia. She was sitting up in the crib in our family bedroom. The vision of this little person with light-coloured hair became imprinted on my mind. I held and treasured that image and the wonder I felt at that moment.

All the time I was growing up I was puzzled. When I saw my sister for the first time, she was beautiful. She had been in our Wideman grandmother's care since she was born.

I was an adult and had children of my own when my baby sister found out who had cared for her for the first six months of her life. Our father went to Hazel, the woman who was our caregiver, when our mother was in the mental hospital. He asked her if he could bring the baby home. Up to that time, she didn't know there was a third little girl.

Hazel was the second girl in an already large family. She told me that she knew this man had come to get her so she could care for his girls. She was hiding and didn't want to go. She had relatives, cousins, in the Markham community where my mother grew up. Austin Weeks was with my dad that day.

I saw Julia on Hazel's knee. As Hazel combed Julia's hair, she exclaimed, "Look at these curls." On that day, there were one or two other adult women at our house. They must have been Hazel's sisters. I would be the observer, the witness, to the events to come. My sisters have no memories of the time when our mother was alive.

When my mother came home from Ponoka, I was with her, but we weren't on the farm with my sisters. First we lived with the family of Reverend Ray Shantz at Markham. They had a son, Wayne, who would leave for school while it was still dark. I think he had to go to Fleet.

One day he was taking matches from the holder on the wall. He held his finger to his lips and said, "Don't tell." He thought the women would be too busy to notice. I looked out the window and saw him lighting matches and dropping them down the well.

I said, "Wayne's got matches. He's dropping them down the well." I hoped it was the water well, not the ice well.

I travelled with my mother to Edmonton. Our picture was taken when we walked down the city street. We went into the store and bought that black-and-white photo. Then my mother and I went to a place that I later learned was where unwed mothers delivered their babies. In the morning, I was to see the babies. The people at the facility said that I'd have to wear a mask because I had a cold. I was ready for the mask, but then they said that a hankie over my mouth would be enough. It was like that first day combing Julia's hair. Some women held the bigger babies and were fixing their hair. In another room, babies were crawling on the floor.

My mother and I also lived on the main street of Castor. Each day she would take me to Dr. Cousineau's house, where she would help the doctor's wife while I played with their children, Elaine and Dick. Elaine was my age; she and I weren't going to school. Dick had a birthday and was ready for the spanking he would receive at school. He told me to try spanking him. He had a tin lid inside his pants. It was rough from the nail holes punched into it.

Sometimes after lunch, the doctor would shave in the bathroom before he went back to work. While at his home, I needed to use the toilet. I was shy, but Elaine said that it was okay because he was a doctor. I was still getting used to flush toilets. I was confused. Something strange was in the toilet. Years later, I realized it was coffee grounds.

The United Church in Fleet was served by a Reverend Rowe from Castor. One Sunday when he was coming to preach, he drove me in his car out to the farm so I could spend some time with my sisters and my father. Hazel was looking after my sisters while I was with my mother.

When we lived in Castor, my tonsils became inflamed and needed to be removed. My mother got me some medicine, but it wasn't Castoria. That was what I had wanted. She said that this other tonic was better for me. After that, I went to hospital—and it was Dr. Cousineau who took out my tonsils.

When I was on the operation table, the doctor showed me something that looked like a flour sifter and then told me to breathe in and count to ten. I think I got to three before I woke up with a sore throat. I could only eat good things like Jell-O and ice cream.

My mother and I went out to her parents' farm when I was recuperating. I was there with my tender throat. On the sideboard, I saw rising white loaves with some whole grains or bran on them. The bread was soft and warm and smelled so good when it came out of the oven.

My maternal grandparents had an interesting way of seeding their garden. Horses would pull the seed drill that was used in the fields. A board was attached to the back of the drill. Two or three women or family members would stand on that board and feed garden seeds into the holes in the grain holder. In this way, the whole garden was planted in a short time.

The doctor's family gave me a treasure: rabbit's fur booties that fit the only doll I ever had.

When I had a temper tantrum and broke the corner off the sewing machine, I thought my real mother was the one who bandaged my head. Much later, I recalled this day and decided who our visitors had been. There were small children and a big woman nursing a baby. I was curious. I hadn't ever seen a baby suckling.

My doll had been sitting on the sewing machine with her booties on her feet. When the company was gone, the booties were gone, too, and I ran in a mad flap and bumped into the bottom corner of the sewing machine with my forehead. I broke off a piece of wood. My mother at the time wrapped a white strip of cloth over my hair and covered the cut on my forehead. I was able to look into the buffet mirror to see what it looked like. I still have a scar in the middle of my forehead.

It took me a long time to figure out that that family was Hazel's. The nursing baby was her mother's 14th child, Ruby, who was younger than my sisters and I. After she covered my wound, Hazel said that she'd put away the booties to keep them clean. I don't remember playing with the rabbits' fur booties after that day.

I remember a photo of my father as a young man holding his Bible to his chest. When I was a teenager, he told me that he was teaching an adult class at Sunday school at Markham Church. He was making sense of a lesson from the book of Revelation. Three Bible school students were present that day. He asked each one to take the lesson. They refused, yet once they came into class, they embarrassed him with their superior knowledge.

He didn't teach Sunday school after that. He found other buddies. One night they were drinking with him in our house. My sisters were asleep and it was dark outside. My mother and I left the house and spent some time crouched in the caragana bushes across the lane. We looked back at the lighted windows. The light was the dim glow of a wick lamp with a glass globe.

I don't know how my mother's thoughts and plans were linked to my father's drinking. My mother's family was opposed to alcohol consumption and saw it as a sin. My sister Joan told me that our father wanted to show off his beautiful wife by taking her to dances, but she wouldn't go. My aunt Muriel was a lifetime member of the Women's Temperance Union.

I later found out that my father was drinking before my mother went to the mental hospital. One day, my father threw dippers full of water from our drinking pail onto my mother. I was with her in the bedroom when she took off her wet clothes. She was wearing the laced-up corset we used to see in the Eaton's catalogue.

When we were little and my mother was still alive, we got it in our heads that we would pray for Daddy to take us to church, maybe even our mother's church at Markham. That next Sunday, our father put on his suit. My mother was standing near the coal bucket on the day my father left for church. He kicked at her as he passed by, saying that she hadn't pressed his suit.

We went to our bedroom and watched him walk down the lane. I held the bedrail as I jumped up and down with joy. We saw him walking to church without us.

I watched my mother doing her projects, which included building a wooden step in front of the outside door so some of the dirt and boots could stay outside. She cut a hole between the two-by-fours to make a shelf in the bedroom. She made a drop-leaf table to put under the south-facing window in the kitchen.

She also made blocks of soap that hardened in a wooden trough that looked like a chick feeder. She used stencils and yellow paint to decorate a wooden fretwork picture frame. The cupboard doors for the kitchen were oilcloth stretched over a wooden frame. Mom used maple leaves dipped in deep maroon paint to decorate those doors. When the design wore off the linoleum floor, my mother dipped scrunched paper into variously coloured paints to replace the pattern.

I had another temper tantrum near the big house where my grandparents and Auntie Doreen lived. There were several nice, shiny cars there, and all the men were wearing suits. I was supposed to stay home. I was stamping my feet because I wanted to ride in one of those cars. Everyone must have been going to a funeral. My mother was dressed up, too. I wanted to go, but I was supposed to stay home. I was stamping my feet and crying or yelling. I was surprised when I got a spanking on my bum from my mother.

She stayed home, too. We might have been driven to Ruby's house. Ruby was my mother's cousin; we spent the day with her. It ended up being a special day because I passed it with these two adult women, all of us looking at Ruby's garden.

One of the buildings near our house must have held the coal for the fire. There was a chicken house there. I went outside to play and found the frozen bottles of water and rosehips that were emblems of my efforts to can. I was imitating my mother's canning by putting rosehips in water inside of old medicine or vanilla bottles. The bottles were on the north side of the house and had frozen overnight.

I had a dream that made me afraid to be outside after dark. In the dream, my sisters and I were outside in the early evening in our white nighties, and Grampa told us to go inside because of some possible danger—like, maybe the bogeyman would get us. Before we got into our house, a big, round, long thing came from its burrow out of the ground to get us. I didn't know what a snake looked like. It really scared me.

When I was almost ready to start school, I was sent across the field alone. I was told, "The cows won't hurt you." There they were in a big, black clump, all of them looking at me. I felt very small. I had to find some courage. Maybe my schoolgirl clothes helped me feel strong. I took one step and then another. Maybe I had been told not to run. I walked across the field toward the grain elevators. I stepped across the gravel road and then across the railroad tracks and into the little town. I don't know how I found the schoolhouse. The other kids there were kind. One of the girls was drawing grapes for me to colour.

One day we went to visit Auntie Doreen because she was making ice cream, which required hours of turning the handle on top of the wooden ice cream maker.

Another time we might have been told to go and visit Gramma. We shyly peeked into the kitchen and saw her seated, working in the round dishpan that was speckled blue on the outside. Gramma held it on her knee. Maybe she was peeling potatoes. She told us that we had to come more often because Auntie Doreen was gone and she was alone.

My mother told me that if we went to sleep in a snowbank, we would wake up with the angels. In winter, our way of moving things around the farm was by using the stone boat, a flat raft of wood dragged by the horses. In my imagination, I saw my mother and myself on that stone boat, sitting in the straw, with angels around us. I guess I thought we would travel with the angels.

There wasn't any snow on the ground on the morning when I looked out to the barnyard and saw the activity there. I think I understood that the sheet on Dr. Cousineau's car held my mother's body. Daddy was with us at the house. A policeman stopped to talk to him, but I'm not sure what was said.

That morning, I was the grownup taking out the chamber pot and emptying it. My auntie, who lived a mile to the west, came to our house to find and iron a dress for my mother to wear in the coffin. She was my father's aunt, and her name was Lydia. Now there were no adult women on the farm. First Auntie Doreen died, then Gramma died, and now my mother had died.

Hazel might have been working at the next farm, but I'm not certain.

I want to tell my sisters about picking rocks, because they were there but don't remember. We were out in the field with Grampa and Daddy, putting stones on the wagon. It was spring in the black, dusty field. We would find the smaller rocks, and the men would lift up the heavier ones. I had taken my shoes off. When we were riding into the yard, I couldn't find the shiny black shoes my mother had bought for me. Grampa and Daddy walked back across the field and found them. I didn't want to lose anything else.

I Go to School

My aunt Helene and my uncle Allan had a daughter, Valera, who was older than I was. They lived far away. My mother and I had visited them. We took a ferry ride across the river, but I had wanted to ride in the smaller boat that was being pulled behind. The ferryman told me that it was too dangerous.

Helene and Allan must have come for the funerals. They did come to the big house to look after us. I was 6, Joan was 5, and Julia was 3. We left the little house and all that our life had been, and we started living in the big house with Grampa and Aunt, Uncle and Cousin. I was watching as Grampa was bouncing my sisters on his knees and singing "Two Little Girls in Blue."

When we were still in the little house, we sang nursery rhymes. One of our favourites was the one with the lyrics, "Baa, baa, black sheep, have you any wool?" Their answer is, "Three bags full." We had to sing each line: one for the master, one for the lady, and one for the little boy who cries in the lane. We all liked the number three. Although we were three good things, I didn't dispute the notion that bad things came in threes, too. Three adult women on our farm died before I went to school.

My sister Joan, who is 11 months younger than I am, and I started school in 1946. We continued the family tradition of beginning school together. Perhaps there was too much turmoil and uncertainty in my family for me to start alone when it was time. My mother had returned from the mental hospital in Ponoka. We lived in Castor for a while. Maybe we had gone back to the farm so Joan and I could go to school together.

Auntie Helene helped us get dressed for that first day. The elementary school was on the east side of the road that ran north from the railway station. That first year we had eight grades in our one-room schoolhouse. It must have been hard to teach that many grades. I think the teacher was new to the profession. She enlisted the cooperation of the older boys by having them do odd jobs around the school. I'm not surprised that our teacher married a young man who lived across the road from the school. She moved away. I don't know if she ever taught school again.

The yard on the west side of the road had two more school buildings for junior and senior high. There were barns in both yards, so a team of horses driven by an older boy could bring one wagon of children from the west and another from the north. One or two could come on a saddle horse or pony. We were close enough to walk in warm weather.

When Joan and I were in Grade 1, Tom and Ted were our classmates. There were eight grades, so there was only so much our teacher could do with us. The four of us would go out to the swings while students in the other grades continued their work. There were two swings for boys and two for girls, so we each had our own swing. The boys would tell us that their dads had guns and would shoot us. I visualized a rain of bullets coming toward us, but we stayed sitting on our swings nonetheless.

Tom had his birthday between Joan's and mine, so he was the closest thing to the brother I wished I had. He had to repeat Grade 1, so his brother, Jim, became his classmate, just as Joan was mine. I had a crush on Ted, but he moved away and I never saw him again.

In Grade 3, I was getting the strap for not doing my arithmetic homework. Home was not a happy place for me. I was falling behind my sister in my studies. She learned to read long before I figured out how to solve that mystery.

I was starting to have some conflicts with the boys, too. The Schokenmier family from west of Fleet had three boys close in age, which paralleled our family of three girls.

One day at noon, I was pestering Alvin. He went into the school and got the long-handled stick with a hook on its end that was used to open the high windows. He came after me and ripped off the fake pocket of my dress. I chased him to the boy's toilet, but I didn't look in.

When the teacher came back after lunch, I knew the other kids were telling her about me. We were in line at the water cooler; Tom was ahead of me. He grabbed a second drink, so I hit him on the head with my tin cup. That finished it. I got the strap.

Stan was a grade ahead of me. I thought I liked him. All I got out of that was kicks in the shins. He was in the other school when I and Tom were in Grades 6 and 5, respectively. Noon hour was our time for physical contests. At the other school, the kids had boxing gloves to use for sparring, but in grade school our contests were mostly tests of strength. Tom and I spent a year apart from one another's company when I was in Grade 7 and he in Grade 6, but we resumed our tussles once he made it to junior high.

Tom would try to pull me around by my hair, and I would grab onto the coat hooks in the cloakroom so he could pull harder. If I tried to fight with younger boys, they would fly into a rage, so I left them alone.

Our New Mama

The day Daddy married Hazel was a school day, March 12, 1947. We were riding the hayrack on sleigh runners, pulled by the team Dago and Stella. Uncle Allan and Grampa told us that Daddy was getting married. We stopped at the little house on the way out of the yard. Daddy came out and talked to us. Hazel looked out the window and waved to us.

I didn't know that Auntie Helene was pregnant and that our twin cousins would be born in June. My aunt and uncle and Valera moved away, and Hazel and Daddy came to live with Grampa and the three of us in the big house. One day, Daddy got us together in the kitchen and told us that we would now call Hazel "Mama."

By the time I attended school, we couldn't depend on the clucky hens, so in April we bought chicks from the hatchery and cared for them under a heated brooder. The brooder had a galvanized roof that kept the heat low enough for the chicks to stay warm without crowding into corners and smothering each other. That brooder was set up in the same little house that had nurtured me as a toddler.

That house was moved into Fleet and became the post office in 1954. It was moved again to the yard that once belonged to Charlie Mills. It stands today in the yard of a new owner. I was pleased to show it to my sisters and their children. It is very small compared to the homes we have today.

Electricity was installed on our farm in 1953, when I was 13. Up until that time, my family handled farm produce, and all the food we ate, in much the same way my grandfather and his family had done since 1905. The first electric lights made homework much easier.

The refrigerator changed how we handled milk, eggs and meat. Before we got a fridge, meat was cut up and wrapped in freezer paper at the butcher's in Castor—and it was stored there until we brought it home in small amounts. In winter, the unheated summer kitchen on the north side of the house was cold enough to keep the meat frozen and protected from our dog and cats. The new International Harvester fridge was installed in the hallway that led to the stairs and the front door that we never used.

There was a cookstove and wood box in a corner of the kitchen. From the woodpile in the barnyard, we brought old boards cut to a comfortable length. Building the fire and getting the oven up to heat for baking bread was a challenge that we had to meet as we grew up. In the winter, coal allowed us a longer-lasting fire that still had to be fed and kept going. At night, we banked the fire by closing the dampers. It would burn slowly and last longer this way.

When we were teenagers, our family installed an oil heater in the living room. Before that, we had a wood and coal heater, which I later rescued from my brother's back step on Grampa's farm. I moved it to the acreage near the Nose Hills to heat the room where my teen sons slept.

My journey through school and to adulthood was fraught with pitfalls and struggles. One of these occurred when two Mennonite missionaries came to our school to teach daily vacation Bible school. They taught us about the Second Coming of Jesus, when all the people who had been saved would be taken up to heaven. The missionaries had a felt board bearing pictures of people. As one person was said to be taken up to heaven, his or her picture would be removed from the board. Two people would be walking. One of them would be taken up, and the other would be left.

I didn't want to be taken up if Daddy and Mama and my sisters weren't taken up at the same time. I thought that my parents might all learn about it when they all came to the church service at the end of Bible school. I didn't believe that I could go to heaven and be with my mother. I knew that in heaven there were many mansions, but the concept was still foreign to me.

I was taught to sing a solo, "God Sees the Little Sparrow Fall," for the final night when my family and the community attended. I might have been 8 years old. I can't remember how I felt as I sang on that final night.

United Church vacation school didn't include what I later learned to refer to as an altar call. Gull Lake Bible Camp, which was organized by the missionary church of my uncle Willie, appealed to us kids because we wanted to learn to swim or at least play in the lake. When I was 12 and 16, we learned Bible verses so we could attend this camp. We went to Evangelical Young People's meetings, which were often held in Castor, to keep us away from dancing. The missionary church represented our mother's religion and that of her surviving relatives. Daddy was the only one who had had a real falling out with that sect, but he made sure that we attended United Church and Sunday school at Fleet every Sunday.

Mama Hazel sewed dresses, pyjamas, aprons and underwear. She would shop from the Eaton's or Simpson's catalogue for coloured bobbysocks in spring and for warm clothes in winter. She sewed clothes for herself and later taught us to sew, knit, embroider and crochet. We even learned smocking.

When our one pair of shoes wore out or we grew out of them, we would draw an outline of one of our feet and send it to the catalogue's order fulfillment centre. One of my shoe sizes was 1; then my feet grew to size 3;

soon thereafter, I wore a 5. But even then my feet hadn't finished growing.

Our first brother, Sheldon, was born in Coronation when I was 10. We were in bed when Daddy came home and phoned Aunt Lydia's husband to tell him that he had a new hired man.

One night I was entrusted with the care of my baby brother. He was supposed to be sleeping in the next room when we went to sleep. I was dreaming about watching a movie and wishing that the baby would stop crying so I could enjoy the show. When I realized that it was my brother crying, I got out of bed and picked him up.

One night we were going to bed by ourselves because our parents had gone out to the movies. It was still light outside as we stood at the top of the stairs looking out at the Nose Hills. Our cat was turning in with us. I reached down and touched her taut, fat belly and said, "She is going to have her kittens soon." My sisters were in the other bed while the cat was sleeping with me. Soon I was hearing a lot of licking and slurping and mewing from under the covers.

When my parents came to go to bed, I said to them, "The cat had her kittens in my bed."

Mom's first response was, "Don't be silly. You don't know what you're talking about."

I threw back the covers, and there was the mother and four little kittens. We put the cat and kittens in a dresser drawer and changed my bed sheets. Then we all went to sleep.

My brothers Patric and Harley were born when I was a teenager. We had plenty of practice looking after them as they grew. Mama thought Joan was better at those tasks than I was. I continued trying to win Mama's approval.

When I was in Grade 12, there were six children and our parents around our supper table. I had a stutter when I tried to speak. I hadn't thought that there was room for me to get a word in edgewise.

The Middle Grades

I often thought how glad I was that we could enjoy the cards, dances, socials and drinking that all made up an important part of our family and community life. When I was a teenager, the boys brought beer when we went for a drive and maybe shot ducks, but they didn't offer any to us. Sometimes they would trade their warm beer for some cold beer of Daddy's.

One of the dances was a box social, for which we prepared decorated lunch boxes. Daddy was told which one was Mom's. We didn't know whose name was put on the other boxes. I hadn't expected anyone to buy my lunch box. When the teacher's son got it, he didn't want to eat lunch with me, so he sold my box to Gus. He was from Lucerne School and knew some of the members of our 4-H club, so I had lunch with him, while Jack Nelson ate lunch with his sister.

We were getting ready for another dance when there was a knock on the front door—the one we never used. I went there and saw that it was Gus. I told him to go to the other door. I went to the kitchen and said, "Mom! It's Gus!"

She said, "Don't be silly."

Gus then appeared at the door we used all the time. "Is Lavera here?" he asked. I was hiding in the hallway.

Mom said, "Johnny? He's down at the barn."

Gus left in his truck. For part of the dance, I sold candy with one of the other girls. Gus was in attendance, but he never asked me for a dance.

On Monday at school, the boys told me, "He was fooling around downstairs and tore his pants."

A popular song we heard at the time was about a poor old wooden Indian who never got a kiss. My friends teased me, "Poor old Gus. He never got a kiss."

When I was 10, I had a red taffeta dress with white embroidery on the chest. I loved that dress and felt like a princess when I wore it.

I sewed my own dresses for the dances when I was a teenager. My father would ruin the enjoyment and excitement, though. When I returned home, I would brace myself for his reprimand.

He would say, "You didn't behave yourself. You were running in and out."

Daddy drank Scotch whiskey until he found that most of his friends preferred rye whiskey. He was offering someone a drink from a bottle of White Horse. I think our visitor was Jack Nelson. He said, "I don't know. That horse has quite a kick," when my father offered him a glass.

When friends or neighbours stopped by, Dad would offer them a drink. They would stand in the kitchen, and he would pour two drinks straight up, no mixer. Eddy English was one of my father's friends. His wife didn't allow drinking in the house, so Eddy stashed bottles around his farmyard. Daddy would be surprised when one of these turned up.

One time, Daddy and another friend were drunk while the rest of us were getting ready for the Christmas concert. Daddy tried to give little Julia a drink, but that was the only time he encouraged any of us to drink. I myself didn't drink alcohol until I left home.

We did have an ice rink that was handy to both the elementary and the junior–senior high school. The school with access to the rink had a 25-minute recess, and the other had a 5-minute recess, so we both used it, but at different times. Our town had the Fleet Flyers hockey team, so the rink featured sideboards and was well maintained. If there was a game at night, we would stand on the snowbanks on the other side of the sideboards and watch. One time a puck hit me in the shin.

Those boards were handy when I was learning to skate. Gradually I was able to move farther and farther away from them and more toward the centre of the ice. When at the rink, we alternated between hockey and free skating, and soon I acquired a warped sliver of a cast-off stick so I could play with the boys. I enjoyed our games. One Friday, Larry and I crashed while coming around the goal crease. We were of equal height at the time, so we had matching black eyes for the weekend.

Mr. J. L. Voloshin was our teacher in junior high up to Grade 10. His wife taught us in the primary grades. In our community, he was labelled The Red. He came to us from Saskatchewan and likely supported the Cooperative Commonwealth Federation (CCF). People called him a communist.

One day in social studies, Joan and I debated with Tom and Jim. We chose the affirmative to the question, "Are immigrants who came from Europe after the war helpful to our community?" Tom and Jim argued that we didn't want or need them. After our class, we went out to the skate shack for our 25-minute recess. All the older kids in Grades 9, 10 and 11 tried to convince Joan and me that we were wrong. I couldn't understand this because we had welcomed the children of the workers on their parents' farms as our classmates. Why weren't the other kids happy to have farm workers? Daddy told Joan not to call these Europeans DPs (short for "displaced persons").

This was the first time I realized that others did not share my political views. My grandfather's political statement was that the suspenders that held up his pants were his Social Security.

Joan devoured books, reading faster than I did. I took five or six years longer than she did before I even read one book the whole way through. I would take a book off the shelf at school. It didn't seem that there were many. I would try to read a paragraph, but I couldn't get into it. Anne of Avonlea's first day in a new school must have triggered discomfort in me. I didn't continue reading it. Now Joan has her young grandchildren riveted to that and other books.

Joan still recommends authors and books to me. I usually read slowly, cover to cover. Joan will go to the back and read the conclusion first.

At some point, I discovered the Pollyanna books. I learned that Pollyanna could always find a positive outcome for many of life's setbacks. If she found a young man who had lost all hope for the future, then she would find some quality in him that would help him move on. There were a number of Pollyanna books, so different authors were found to follow the formula or theme of the previous books.

My favourite thing to read was the *Star Weekly,* which had pictures I liked to look at. Joan would tell our sister Julia and me bedtime stories. We would be in our beds while Joan related entire books to us. The adventures of the English young men who went off to North Africa in the French Foreign Legion finally got my attention. I wanted to follow them myself. I read all three of those books. I handed in a book review of one of them. That book review was 13 handwritten pages long.

Life on the Farm

I found a ditch of water that was teeming with water creatures and in which I could wade or else sit beside on a stone. I let the mud squish around my toes. It was my special place, but I was found out when I got slough itch on my calves. I would wander through the pasture looking for little patches of wild strawberries, those delicate, juicy blobs of red. I brought some home in a dish for jam. Mama said there wasn't enough for jam.

Calling the cows home was another adventure. They might have been in the middle of a slough, in which case we'd have to throw rocks to convince them to start home. Another time they hid in the trees at the far end of the south field.

We had a muddy dugout in the north pasture. One time we were playing in it, likely without permission, and I was riding an old log across the water. I didn't know how to swim. I tried to touch bottom. When I didn't find it, my leg went into a cramp. The bottom of the dugout was just beyond my reach. The experience scared me.

I had an even worse experience when we were at the Stromes' dugout. I was enjoying the rubber tube until Danny took it away from me at the far end. I walked along the side of the dugout and thought I was close enough to the shallow end; I stepped in from the side.

This dugout was deeper than the one at home. I took one step too many and was soon in over my head and drowning. I think Walter pulled me out. I wanted to know why it had taken him so long, as it seemed long to me. He had been quick to see what had happened.

Another summer adventure I enjoyed occurred when I spent a week with Mom's sister Dora and her husband, north of Castor. This was special because I went without my sisters or other family. I was their kid for a week before their girls were born. Dora had an organ. We would come in from working outside, and she would sing and play "Bringing in the Sheaves."

Grampa kept some hives of bees in the trees that bordered the north edge of our garden. We were all at the barnyard as Mama and Daddy were milking the cows. When we let the cows out into the field, we noticed some bees flying around us.

We were carrying the pails of milk to the house and were almost to the house yard when I was stung on my forehead, really close to my eye. We all went back to the safety of the barn. When Mom looked at my sting, she found that the bee had left its stinger. Grampa continued to work with the bees while we waited at the barn.

When it was finally safe to go to the house, we found many dead bees on the windowsills of the summer kitchen. The bees' stingers were embedded in the wood. We were told that they would die without their stingers. Grampa controlled the bees by calming them with the smoke he made from a smouldering fire inside a little box, which he could squeeze to force out the smoke. I think he had to kill the bees that had gotten into the house.

Learning to milk the cow was also a special adventure for me because it was time I spent alone with Daddy. The cows stood in the yard and let us milk them. There were six. I started to learn on Dolly. She was gentle and patient, as her name suggests. Daddy would milk all the others while I struggled with Dolly. Later, I got fast enough to start on Socks before my dad finished with the other cows.

Mama found the old ice cream maker stored in the summer kitchen. She brought it out. We were adding ice and then salt to make the ice colder. And then came all the turning, turning and turning of the handle. We used our own farm cream and eggs to make the ice cream. The smooth, cold and good-tasting finished product was worth the effort.

If we found Ray Davey on our visits to Fleet on days when we didn't have school, he would give us a nickel to go to Wings Store for an ice cream cone. One day I hopped along the wooden sidewalk and dropped my nickel between the boards. We would also take the pop bottles we found along the road and exchange them for two cents at Wings'. Beer bottles had to be taken to Mac's Store. We tended to be embarrassed because there were always people there, usually men, and Mac was always so busy that it was hard to get his attention. Plus, we were doing this for a mere two cents.

Poplar Trees

Beginning when I was 10 years old, my siblings and I were in 4-H Beef Club. Leo Slemp was one of the club leaders driving some of us on a tour of our club mates' farms. We were showing off our baby beef calves. Leo pointed out some young poplars in a field near his farm and told me that there hadn't been any trees there before the dust bowl days of the 1930s, which were accompanied by prolonged drought.

The twigs that started those trees had blown in from somewhere else and had grown when the rains came. Forty-five years later, these small groves, or patches, of wild poplars were falling down.

The town of Castor had planted a variety of cultivated poplar trees along the main boulevard and on many other streets. Workers extended the poplars' lives by pruning them yearly. Some of the poplars that had been planted down the centre of the street in Castor have since been removed and replaced by spruce trees.

I learned that the Bank of Montreal in Castor is now the Battle River Credit Union. The Bank of Montreal had occupied the brownstone building that was torn down when the new bank was built. The credit union took over the new building. Recently, I admired three of the surviving thick, heavy poplar trunks. They showed the evidence of their years of pruning. Great round growths were left when suckers were cut out of the sides of the trees. Each tree is aged and wrinkled but still vigorous and alive. Their trunks have too large of a circumference for me to wrap my arms around.

Like a prairie poplar, I myself have been severely pruned back and am very hardy because of it. With the words *pruned back,* I am referring to the trauma I experienced when first my mother died, and then when my first husband, Dave, died. Twelve years after Dave passed, my second husband died.

Prairie Weather

As a young child, I learned about weather when my canning bottles froze. We had to be cautious of the cold when we were travelling to and from school. If Grampa took us with the team, he might heat a brick on the stove and wrap it in paper so we could huddle around it, beneath a blanket, while we rode in the wagon. A baby pig, lamb or calf might be brought to the house to warm itself on the coldest days.

Some days we would walk across the field to school. I wore stockings held up by garters. There was bare skin above my stockings. One day, the coldness caught me by surprise, and for the last stretch of our journey through the town, I walked on legs that felt wooden from the cold.

Even when we had a truck ride into the town, I felt cold against its door. It seemed I was always hunched against the cold. Daddy might take a pan of ashes from the stove to heat the motor enough to get it started. Some years, Daddy left our truck parked at the highway so that if someone came through with a team or a tractor, he or she could drive it to Castor or Coronation.

Before television weather reports and televised entertainment were available, we watched Mother Nature's show from our upstairs west window. We'd behold the flashes of lightning with confidence that the two lightning arresters on the high pitch of our roof would ground the electricity. I don't know if the radio ever gave us any indication of coming storms. The thermometer outside our door was consulted regularly, and sometimes the *Farmer's Almanac* was helpful, too.

We had a big blizzard that lasted three days but which had started with a sudden thaw. Late that night, Daddy had learned that the temperature was 32°F. Over the next few days, the snow swirled around the house; we couldn't see anything. We didn't go outdoors. After the storm was over we learned the Willis family was away visiting their father on the coast of British Columbia. Joe Makaruk was looking after their cattle. In the middle of the storm, he walked the three miles south from his home in Fleet and back, having to keep the fence posts in view so as to find his way. Eddy and Gladys English survived three days in their car.

After the blizzard, we missed school because the roads had yet to be cleared of snow. The farmers were using a snow blower they had bought together, but the work was slow going because the snow was higher than the tractor in places. My sisters and I took our toboggan up to the Nelson place to see how they were progressing. While the tractor worked below, we stood on the bank, breaking off chunks of snow. I dropped my toboggan; the men had to move it before they continued their work.

One winter, the snow came to stay before the threshing was done. Two brothers, gold miners from Yellowknife, helped us to dig the stooks out of the snow for threshing.

In the summer of a different year, we experienced a windstorm that sent the dust swirling, which blotted out the landscape. The storm had come on gradually. The first indication was the dust gathering on our windowsill. At one point, we saw the entire sheep shed float from behind the barn only to land where the slough had been in the spring. When the storm was over, we had a chance to assess the damage. The ventilator from the top of the barn had landed in a heap in the middle of our yard and looked like a damaged house. A granary out in the field was flattened.

We didn't have electricity at that time, but the power lines in Fleet were lying on the ground. Mike Checkel married Jean Griffiths two weeks earlier. The roof had blown off their stone house during the windstorm.

Sometimes in the spring we would walk out to the end of the lane and scoop a pail of water out of the ditch. There might be some tadpoles in it. In any event, we all enjoyed the soft water for washing our hair. One evening, the rain was pouring down and the rain barrel was overflowing. I was at home alone and didn't want to lose the precious water, so I ran back and forth—getting soaked in the process—to bring in the water. I filled the reservoir on the back of the cookstove, and then I filled the copper canning tub. My family came home before I got completely carried away.

When I went to university and studied the music of the piece entitled *Sorcerer's Apprentice*, I was reminded of my water-carrying episode.

We kept the cookstove for a long time after we got electricity because that selfsame stove heated water for our laundry and baths.

We used water from the well for drinking, cooking and washing. The well was near the spot where Hazel's home sits. The older girls in the Charles family gave us some nice dresses after they grew out of them. One day I was wearing a dress that fit me quite nicely. I was beginning to develop a bit of a figure. We needed a pail of water and, since there had been a recent rain, I went to fetch it in my bare feet. I was walking to the well when I saw a basin-size puddle that looked just right for soaking my feet in. I put on the brakes, slipped on the slick clay soil and went right down on my bum into that puddle.

One of my first practice teaching assignments in Edmonton was to give a lesson about weather. I and the class were talking about clouds and rain when the sun came in so strong that the teachers watching me had to pull the blinds. After the lesson, my instructor wanted to know why I hadn't talked about the weather forecast on television. I didn't have a television or watch the one that was downstairs where we roomed. It wasn't part of my experience.

Teen Troubles

When I was a teenager, I was haunted by my stepmother's name-calling. She'd refer to me as a cow's tail or as a slowpoke. She would say in one breath, "You are going to have to leave," and in the next she'd ask, "How will you survive on your own?"

We were told we couldn't date until we were 18. Our parents didn't give us much direction for how to start dating. In addition, I think that the townspeople's gossip was used as a way to control us. We didn't want to be the ones who had people talking. Some of our classmates were pregnant when they married. My stepmother's young sister Beatrice seemed to have a better understanding of the pitfalls experienced by two couples who went skinny-dipping.

When my sisters and I were leaving home, my father said, "Now you are on your own. You are responsible for your life."

In my young life, I had thought that Mom was ignoring me all the times when she didn't answer me. I think, now, that she simply couldn't hear me. She had dropped out of school when she had developed an ear infection. When I complained of aches and pains, she would tell me that I was as healthy as a horse. When my sisters were sick with measles or chickenpox, they were feverish and sick in bed. While they were covered with chickenpox, I had an easier time of it. I had two spots that I picked so much, I should have scars in those places. Mosquitoes left terrible welts on me, which I picked and scratched, too.

My teen years were difficult for me and my stepmother. We had many fights, mostly arguing and shouting matches. Mom would say something that helped me understand how difficult her life was. She felt that the community was watching her, and also that people were critiquing her performance as a stepmother.

Later in life, I did finish reading *I Was a Step-Child* by Clarence Boon. In that story is a young woman who had lived during the World War II era and had lost both her parents before she was 17. She leaves her mean stepmother and survives a lonely journey across the prairie to find a new life and eventually marry. As I read the book, I felt compassion for this young woman and for myself. My grief is still with me. I am very familiar with emotional pain and am able to feel the pain of others when I read their stories.

I think the Willis family had some sympathy for my plight when they asked me to help with housework in the summer after I had finished Grade 9. Jessie was pregnant and already had a baby who was still in diapers. The couple had a son, Dick, and a daughter, Bonnie, both of whom were not as close in age as this baby and the one they were expecting. Jessie was happy to have the help of a teenager who had experience with babies.

I enjoyed my work with, as well as the acceptance and encouragement I felt from, the Willises. They treated me more like an adult companion, which mimicked the relationship I had had with my birth mother. Dennis and Jessie were fascinating people who took an interest in me. In addition, they paid me a little money I could call my own.

I was excited to receive my marks and know I had passed Grade 9. Joan would later be awarded the Governor General's Award for her marks. I needed to be recognized for myself.

High School

Castor had two schools. One was Catholic-attended and supported by French families. The priest there encouraged people to have large families. That school is running to this day, even though now fewer people in Castor speak French. When we finished nine grades at Fleet, we moved on to attend the Castor Public School for high school. Gus Wetter was our school board chairman, but Gus Wetter School had not yet been planned and built.

High school in Castor was a new challenge. Most of our classmates had been in classes together since Grade 1. We were from Fleet and didn't feel accepted or welcomed. We had to try to make new friends. Three boys came from Bulwark, and Gayle Gilchrist came from Beaver School, where her father had been her teacher for an extra year. She was in Grade 11. She was a caring and considerate person who helped me with my difficulties. I was reassured to discover that others were new as well.

We also had to meet the expectations of our teachers. Some marked our essays with low marks. Their tests covered more pages in our textbooks than we were used to. For the first few months, we were in shock.

The next year we had to write a report from an outline, the topic of which we had to choose and the items of which we had to prepare in point form. I couldn't think of a topic, and I found it difficult to get a feel for the format. I was supposed to be working on it over the Remembrance Day holiday.

I decided to go with my family to car bingo in Coronation. I saw people looking at each other, hoping that no one else would be the first to call bingo. This social event had a much different feel to it than our box socials, dances and candy sales to raise money for our clubs. People brought much less community spirit to bingo.

I named my essay "Bingo Fever." I was able to make a case for other forms of fund-raising. I thought this new idea was a sickness. I was able to write passionately on the subject. My teacher, Jack McFetridge, liked it so much that he thought I should have it published in the *Castor Advance.*

If my father could have had education beyond high school, it would have meant a lot to him. He left high school just before completing Grade 12, since his father needed help planting his crops. I think my dad always regretted his lack of further education. There was never any question that his three daughters would finish high school and continue on to university.

On the day Joan and I graduated from high school, we were released early so we could get ready and put on our graduation dresses. Daddy came to town to take us home. He sent us home with the truck while he stayed with his drinking buddies at the bar. He was celebrating because his two daughters didn't graduate every day.

I was angry and upset because Dad needed to get ready for the banquet and ceremonies. I didn't want to be late, and I also didn't know when one of his neighbours would bring him home. I certainly didn't want to be embarrassed by my drunken father at my graduation. When I complained to Mom, she said it wasn't any of my business.

Sometimes Dad would be away at chore time because he knew we could milk the cows by ourselves. When we were in high school, we had milking machines to do the milking. The machines hung on straps around the cow's belly. When one was full of milk, it felt very heavy when we took it away to dump the milk. On school mornings, our dad would take over before we were finished so we could get ready for the school bus.

He encouraged our education, but he also pressed us into service as boys to care for and handle the animals and bring in the harvest. In his eyes, the fact that we were girls didn't limit our opportunities. We did face limitations when it came to our choice of occupations, however. In our narrow experience, we had two choices: nurse or teacher. We had no idea what a social worker was. Women could be missionaries and likely wouldn't marry. Boys or men could be ministers of the church, but girls and women could not.

Community activities included our United Church's Sunday school, vacation school and CGIT (Canadian Girls in Training). My religious and spiritual confusion required me to engage in a constant balancing act. Today, I remind myself that I have to look within and search my own soul—and be the person I want to be, doing the things I want to do. I still inflict on myself the judgment to which I was subjected in my early life. The critical voices continue to pummel me because I learned to be critical of myself. Those messages of my not being good enough continue to resound, long after my critics have passed on.

Review

My mother was taken to a mental institution after her third daughter was born. I was 3. No one ever told me how I reacted to her absence, and I don't remember. When my mother came home after being away for a year and enduring shock treatments and other procedures, I stayed with her while Hazel cared for my sisters. I was a grownup companion to my mother when I was 4 and 5 years of age. At least I felt like a grownup. Mom and I helped the minister's family and the doctor's family, but no one told me that keeping her company would simultaneously help my mother feel better about being out of the mental institution.

My birth mother might still be alive if she had divorced my father. She came home from the mental hospital to find that Hazel had stepped into her role as mother to my sisters and me and as companion to my father. At that time divorce was not considered an option.

I recently read about a man who had received shock treatments for a mental illness and who had also committed suicide. The story suggested that the person had lost parts of his memory as a result of the treatments. I'm sure my mother was given shock treatments.

When my mother was still alive, she and I moved back to the farm where my father and sisters lived—which is where I lived while my mother was away. Hazel was not on the farm at that time. That morning, I looked out to see activity in our barnyard. My mother went there every morning and evening to milk the cow and bring the warm milk back to us. The doctor's car was outside, and there was something wrapped up in a sheet and tied to its roof. Mom hadn't kept her promise to me. I knew that she had left without me, even after saying that we would wake up with angels if we went to sleep in a snowbank.

I treasure memories of my mother. I would like to know more about her. I have read many books about suicide, and I have attended workshops focused on healing from the grief of death and suicide. Suicide is not an answer. It is a question. Every suicide leaves many questions unanswered, and each individual suicide leaves different questions behind. Suicide isn't an answer to life's problems.

No one would talk to me about my mother. I hungered for information about her. I looked to people who knew her. I thought that the doctor's wife and the minister's wife looked like her. They were still alive after my mother died.

I found out that my mom had worked for Mrs. Hallet before she was married. I was glad to have two of Mrs. Hallet's daughters as friends. Later in life they showed me the benefits of divorce. Sometimes it is a necessary choice. When I registered as an adult widow to go to a workshop with Muriel James, I thought she looked just like my mother, too. I was still looking for my mother.

I tried another way of understanding my mother's mental illness. I registered for summer school to take an anthropology class at the University of Alberta in Edmonton. This was after my first husband died and my children were spending the summer with their father's brothers on their farms. The course examined cultural causes of mental illness. I noted differences between the Irish concepts of fairies and magic and the German Mennonite teachings of my mother's family. My maternal grandfather was a fanatical evangelical Pentecostal. I also began looking at difficulties in my parents' marriage. I still wrestle with the religious conflict my parents introduced into my young life.

While I have tried to run away from the hurt and sadness, it follows me and influences my life. I look for ways to move on. I have distanced myself from my story and have created new lives for myself. My story has sent me on a voyage of discovery and exploration, but it does not change who I am. I circle back. I try to be good enough, only to be hurt again when I see injustice and humankind's inhumane treatment of humankind. Out in the world, I have been a foot soldier with a mission.

Striking Out on My Own

When I was finishing high school, my Wideman grandparents were living in their house in Castor and planning their 50th wedding anniversary ("If I live that long," Gramma would say). The night before this event, I stayed over with them so I could help or just be on hand. They had an open house so their friends and neighbours could attend.

During my first summer out of school, I was waitressing on Edmonton's south side while rooming with our stepmother's sister who was married to a missionary minister. I learned that I could handle myself quite well amidst the bantering and flirting and teasing that went on between truck drivers and oil workers and waitresses. I worked in two different restaurants.

The first one was the Top Hat, which didn't have many customers and where there was only one other waitress. She told me that I wouldn't want to work at the other restaurant because I was slow like she was. One day, one of the girls from Frankie's Restaurant stopped on her way to work. She said that Frankie had left and that Betty was the boss now. I should ask Betty for a job, the waitress suggested.

When I went to work at Frankie's, the restaurant was really busy. There were a number of waitresses on each shift. The other waitresses helped me make grilled cheese and grilled chicken sandwiches and banana splits. The time went fast. Frankie's was open 24 hours a day. The graveyard shift started at 11:00, at which time some intoxicated people would turn up. Betty never asked me to take that shift. It was bad enough that I had to catch a bus late at night.

While I was working at Frankie's, I met Ray, who had a motorcycle. I developed a taste for blueberry pie a la mode. Ray worked in maintenance at the tuberculosis sanatorium. One of his co-workers lived near the university in a house with upstairs bedrooms that he rented to students. Joan and I rented the room for $35 a month.

My first year at university brought some challenges. One day I went home at noon and got my mail only to find a letter from the School Division threatening to withdraw my bursary. There was a letter from Student Services suggesting that I could attend classes that taught one how to study. I sat through my psychology class—the only class I shared with my sister Joan—and planned my return to Castor, where I would get a job with the bank. When I told Joan and her friend that I was quitting school, they laughed and continued on to their next class.

Lawrence Radcliff took the time to sit with me in the student lounge and listen to my concerns. He convinced me to get some help and continue with my studies. He was also instrumental in encouraging me to let my name stand as a candidate for Student Parliament, operating as a member of the CCF. Grant Notley was the leader of our campus's CCF party. He later became a much-appreciated member of the Legislative Assembly of Alberta as an Opposition member. When I wore the CCF button around the university, it reminded me of the television program *I Was a Communist for the FBI*.

During my first two years at University of Alberta in Edmonton, I attended one Bible study presented by the Varsity Christian Fellowship. I decided that the organization was too rigid for me. They offered complicated explanations for what I thought was a very straightforward Bible passage. My embarrassment may have paralleled my father's in years past. A theology student from St. Stephen's United Church called me a pantheist because I said that I saw God's glory in nature.

I enjoyed my participation in the Student Christian Movement, and my sister and I attended young people's groups at three United churches near the university.

In our single room, Joan and I cooked on a single-burner hotplate. Meal making was hit-or-miss. Mom sent some canning and jam. My favourite was Rogers Golden Syrup and store-bought white bread. By Christmas, I had gained 20 pounds and stirred up Cecile Bresett's curiosity.

When I was still in high school, Cecile had dropped in for a little visit one Saturday morning. I watched her eyes pop out of her head when she saw my hair in curlers. After she went home, she phoned and asked us to come over for supper that night. As we went into her house, I was lagging behind the rest of my family. Cecile asked where I was before I had gotten into the house.

When we children were leaving home, our stepmother started finding her way. She talked about the clothes she could finally buy for herself. She got her driver's licence and found work in Castor or Coronation and earned some money.

Summer Work Again

In the summer of 1959, after one year at university, I worked at Naramata on the Okanagan Lake. My first trip through the mountains had been memorable. Big Bend Highway, which was to run through Golden, was still under construction, so my bus drove over the Cascade Mountains. The driver had to slowly turn and manoeuvre the bus on the hairpin road that descended one of the mountains. I could see the edges of the road and, beyond them, a long decline. At the bottom was a valley with a little farm. We met the other bus, which was coming east, at which point the two drivers stopped for a rest and visited with each other before they continued their perilous drives.

My sister Joan has her own story of Naramata because she worked there in the summer before when I worked in Edmonton.

In 1959 I had come to Naramata to be on summer staff between my two years of university. Summer staff ate under a tarp outside the kitchen and dining room. New buildings were under construction, so we took coffee breaks with some of the carpenters. Our communication with them was always positive. They would ask us, "Are you winning today?" They were asking if we were achieving what we intended. They were telling us we were worthy. This was how older workers encouraged younger workers.

In Naramata, I pulled weeds in the garden, thinned and picked and then canned peaches and apricots, walked to the post office to get the mail, and worked in the print shop. One day, Bob McLaren asked me to help him repair paddle boards with fibreglass. This gave me another big boost of self-esteem.

I learned to swim at Naramata. Because Alberta lakes are really cold, I hadn't had much opportunity to learn to swim before that time. Spending one week during two different summers at Gull Lake Bible Camp hadn't been enough time or provided me with enough opportunity to learn the skill. When I attended that camp, I was 13 and 16, and there was no formal swimming instruction. At Naramata, Terry White was lifeguard to the children during the day. When our work was done for the day, summer staff had a swim before supper. Terry helped me overcome my fear of deep water and taught me how to swim.

Auntie Minnie and Grampa

When my summer work was finished, I boarded a bus for Quesnel. I travelled all night. Someone said that the lights of Kamloops spelled the town's name on the hill above it. I saw the spread of lights over the hills, but the name wasn't that clear. I paid attention to Clinton because one of the summer staff girls had been raised there. Hundred Mile House was an interesting name. I later found that towns with the word *house* in their name had been Hudson's Bay posts.

I arrived in the morning, and Auntie Minnie picked me up from the bus station. Her family lived in a community named Dragon Lake. Grampa had his own place, but I didn't see it.

He took his sheep with him when he moved there nine years earlier. I think Minnie had her own sheep and made and sold hundreds of wool quilts. Uncle John worked at a plywood factory, so Minnie did most of her own building around their farm.

The rain poured through the roof of Auntie Minnie's addition, which might have been more aptly called a lean-to. It rained so hard that we were told the bus to Prince George was cancelled. But I had a train to catch. Auntie Minnie found out that I could fly to Prince George. I was 19, and Prince George was a lumberjack town, so Grampa Sam flew with me so we could spend the day together, as my train didn't leave until 10:00 p.m. It was the first time either of us had flown. Grampa said he was happy to go home on the bus.

The train station was a safe place, so Grampa left me in the waiting room. I'm glad we had that opportunity to fly, because he overcame his fear of flying and in 1963 he boarded an airplane and flew to Ireland. He skipped my wedding to do so. His one surviving sibling, Mariah, died while he was there. Sixty-two years earlier, he had come to America by steamship.

On the train, I met another university student. He worked in forestry all summer. As the train wound its way back to Edmonton, he pointed out the different kinds of trees. He showed me cedars, pines, fir and spruce. I thought they all looked like Christmas trees. It was the first time I was shown individual trees, not just the forest.

One of the other young women on summer staff, Sue Miller, trimmed my hair. When I got back to university, it was time for photos. I went to the washroom, combed some water through my hair and went for my sitting. I think it was the moist B.C. air and not the haircut that left me with piles of curls in that photo. I'd avoided the practice of winding my wet hair into tight rounds and securing it with bobby pins to make pin curls.

There is a difference between bobby pins and hairpins. I mention this because I described the mountain roads as having hairpin turns. My mother's cousin Muriel and my father's sister Helene were both married to evangelical ministers. I'm not sure if their religion dictated their hairstyles, but they both wore their hair very long and braided into single plait that wound around the top and back of their heads. This braid was held in place with hairpins that were open, not tight like the bobby pins that held our pin curls. A hairpin turn is a tight U-turn that switches back and runs parallel to the road just travelled. On roads with these turns was the only way for busses and vehicles to traverse the steep mountainsides.

Teaching at Brownfield

When I was teaching at Brownfield, my family built a bathroom in the downstairs bedroom that had been Grampa's. Each weekend when I went home, I would expect to see the plumbing installed and functional. I was disappointed on many weekends, however, because the bathroom wasn't yet ready to use. When I had been little and growing up, we bathed on Saturday night. After heating the water on the stove, we took our baths in the round galvanized bathtub in the middle of the kitchen floor. On the day I graduated from high school, I bathed in that galvanized tub.

On one of those weekends, I had gone to the farm and Joan had met me at the door to show me her engagement ring. I was incredulous. I asked her, "Who?" She took my hand and led me to the living room. I thought that Zahid had moved back to Pakistan. I thought there might be someone else. But no. Joan and Zahid were married in June 1961. Julia and I were bridesmaids, and my boyfriend at the time took photos. Joan was ahead of me again. She married a university student—indeed, a very accomplished student who was a highly intelligent engineer.

I went on some dates while at university. Afterward, the guy would normally say he'd call me, but I would never hear from him again. The school held dances, and we were all learning to jive. Usually a boy would ask us for a dance. We were all strangers. We would try to get the hang of this new dance, the jive. If we didn't manage very well, then the boys would drop us off with the other girls and try again with someone else. After a while, we all got better at the jive and spent more time on the dance floor. At Brownfield, some of the younger people, I among them, did the jive, but the old-time dance styles of waltz and foxtrot were still in vogue. Everyone was astonished when the butterfly made it to our country dances. The men liked it. Sometimes they were a little too enthusiastic when tossing the girl in the middle to the other partner.

I also attended some parties and spent some weekends in the city while I was teaching at Brownfield. Gayle Gilchrist was continuing her education and starting her career as a counsellor and social worker. I would stay with her on those occasions. Gayle went on to do tremendously important work as a professor of social work in both Edmonton and Calgary.

The Ranch House
and the Rancher

My first husband, Dave, and I had both separately moved to Brownfield in 1960, which is where we met. I was teaching Grade 5 in May and June, and then I taught Grade 6 for two years. I was dating and curling with someone else when I noticed Dave curling out on the ice, but I didn't yet know who he was. By this time, I knew most of the regular curlers. Some of us were checking the curling schedule as we left the curling rink. Dave signalled that he was single by asking us if we knew of any dances in the area that he might attend.

On another night, Bob Barnes was teasing or joking when he said that Dave had plenty of change in his pockets— that he could change anything but a married woman's name. I noticed Dave again. The other relationship I had been in ended, and I began to see Dave at the dances. He would invite me to dance by asking if he could borrow my carcass. Obviously, he could be colourful with language. Also, he was fairly shy. I told him that he didn't treat me like the dead body of a cow.

In those days, the way for young people to meet was at the dances. The floors in the small halls of Brownfield, Talbot and Silver Heights were filled every time a dance was sponsored by the hall's committee, the 4-H or a students' union. At that time, Brownfield School was consolidated, and students for all 12 grades were bussed in from all the other communities. Talbot and Silver Heights still had stores and community halls. Dances were attended by teenagers as well as the young men who worked on the farms, as some stayed on the farm to work with their fathers, like my father had. There were more single men than women, so I didn't sit out many dances. The other two young women who taught with me and lived with me in the teacherage had been my classmates in high school. They left for Castor right after school every Friday and never participated in community events.

Asking for a dance was easier than asking to take someone home. When I was a teenager, many times boys had asked to take me home from the dances. I always had to get my parents' permission. Since most of the guys were from another town and older than I was, my parents' answer was always no.

At Brownfield, Richard and Marie were two of my friends. They lived near the ranch that Dave was operating, and they were friends with Joe and Anna, both of whom knew Dave because he sometimes came to their place to use the phone. One night, Joe and Richard bet Dave that he wouldn't ask me out. I was hoping he would ask before someone else did. Dave won the bet and asked me out—which was also the first time Dave had asked to take me home. We all celebrated by going to Richard and Marie's for steaks after the dance.

When curling was finished, Dave and I began dating—in the spring of 1962. Sometimes Dave would say that he would pick me up on Friday night. I would wait and wait. I'd look down the road, watching for his truck. He didn't have a phone. He would be rounding up and working with his cattle, which was the reason for his delay.

Dave was baptized and became a member of the United Church as a young person. As a single schoolteacher in my new community of Brownfield, I was working with others to move a small church from the nearby town of Bulwark. I hoped that Brownfield would have a community church like the one I attended as a child, where Dave and I were later married. I was one of the first members of the Brownfield United Church Women.

Dave had a suit he had bought at age 15 when his oldest brother had gotten married. It was navy blue with a shadow of white stripe. When I wanted him to come as my guest to the Brownfield School graduation, he tried to tell me he didn't have a suit. He was shy at public events, so it took some convincing, but he did end up coming. He wore that suit to church, as well. Soon he had worn it for me more times than he had in the 15 years prior, when he wore it only for weddings and funerals.

Dave's ranch was on the south side of the Battle River Valley. We grew up knowing the river. Once we went on a school picnic at Lorraine Bridge. Lorraine was an appealing destination because its landscape provided relief from the flat, empty prairie to the south. There was a large butte we all had to climb. We could also roll up our pant legs and splash in the shallows of the river. The river valley at the ranch featured a hill we called "the butte."

Dave came from the north line of towns, having grown up on a farm near Hardisty. I came from the south line of towns. Brownfield never did have a railroad. It was between the two railroads and highways.

Also, Dave was from a family of eight. He and his brother Donald were the only ones who were single, so those two had lots of nieces and nephews who especially loved Dave. He enjoyed them, as well, and was always handing out Dentyne gum to them.

Dave's family had been stricken by tragedies in the recent past. Both parents had died, and his one sister, Doris, was widowed. They were pulling together, supporting each other and establishing new family gatherings. They often went to Doris's home where her two sons and daughter would play with their cousins.

The family had built a new house for their mother because she was such a great source of inspiration to all of them. They had been very poor, and their mother held this family of eight together throughout the hard times. When the five sons began farming, the farm was heavily mortgaged. When other farmers were selling their horses and buying tractors, Dave's family was using horses to pull machinery.

Dave was 10 years older than I and a child of the 1930s. His family earned some much-needed money by cleaning the school. Farm chores occupied Dave's time and energy before and after school. By Grade 9, he was falling asleep in class and so dropped out to work with his brothers. They asked their neighbours about horse handling and farming practices. When they did get a tractor, they took it to new land they had acquired at Irma and Fabian.

Dave's oldest brother married the teacher who had come to teach at their school. That was around the same time Dave left school. Dave and Donald were the two siblings whose ages fell in the middle. At one point, Donald was farming at Irma and got himself caught up in a piece of machinery's power takeoff. He was near death when a farmer found him. Donald survived, and with great determination he learned to use his two artificial arms and one prosthetic leg. Dave told me that if he ever felt discouraged, he had only to think of all that Donald had experienced and accomplished.

On many Sundays, the family gathered at one of their farms. Allan and Irene were on the home farm where Dave had worked. He moved away from his family when he and his brother-in-law, Ken, bought the Milham place on the south side of the Battle River, around the same time I started teaching. They named it Crystal Springs Ranch. It took Dave and me two years to meet and to get together. I would soon learn that there were springs far away in the pasture where it slopes down to the river and another one in the barnyard. The cattle drank from those springs. I was fascinated by the hilly land covered with groves of aspens and poplars. There were also white paper birch, spruce and patches of wild Saskatoon berries.

As we were driving to one of these Sunday gatherings, Dave was fretting that we were going to be late. I asked him who was usually the last to arrive. Brian and Bessie had the most distance to cover, and their children were young, so Dave said that they would be the last to get there. As we neared the farm, I told him that they were just arriving now, so we wouldn't be too late. I also went over the names of Doris's and Iris's kids—and all the nieces and nephews—so that I would be prepared. I soon found myself reminding Dave of their names.

One sister was married to a fireman in Edmonton. On weekends, they went to Half Moon Lake, where they ran a resort. Dave took me there to meet his sister and her family.

When I met Iris, I was impressed by her beautiful hair. It was long and curly and of a shiny russet colour. She and Ken had a home in Hardisty where Ken owned and ran the B–A gas station that delivered fuel to all of the farms. Hardisty hosted the Canadian Professional Rodeo Association's two-day rodeo every June. There was a dance on Friday and Saturday nights. The rodeo grounds were beside Hardisty Lake, and they sloped down to the outdoor arena. Cars and trucks would park all over the hill. Dave had been helping in the chutes for many years. He really didn't care about other sports, but he often talked about Kenny McLean and Winston Bruce. Rodeo cowboys, stock contractors and chuck wagon drivers were his buddies.

When I had first met Dave, I had already been accepted by the Edmonton Public School Board for a position teaching a special class for slow learners. I had to apply early to be accepted in Edmonton. I was already a little late when I applied. I said that the position was acceptable because I liked helping the difficult students. Dave wanted me to give up the job, but I wanted to stay another year in Edmonton because Julia, my youngest sister, would be my roommate. Joan and her husband had moved to Calgary. In those years when my sisters and I were all pursuing higher education, there was always two of us, but never three, living in that city.

Many weekends I spent on the bus from Edmonton to Camrose, and all along Highway 13 to Hardisty. I had the sequence of the towns memorized. It was a long ride because we stopped in every town to drop off or pick up passengers. Dave would meet me in Hardisty. I already knew all the towns on Highway 12 because I had taken the bus to Castor while I was going to university. Sometimes I would travel to Fleet to visit my family.

Dave and I would go horseback riding. I didn't have cowboy boots, so the stirrups hurt my ankles. One day, we borrowed a pair of work boots from the bunkhouse. I had a camera that we used to take pictures. If Dave used the camera to take a picture of me on horseback, he might cut off the horse's head or tail. I was the inexperienced rider who couldn't keep the horse still, and he was the inexperienced camera operator. One day he was riding a beautiful sorrel horse and wanted to take a picture of me atop it. When I got on, he told me that if the horse went to move, I must jump off. He later sold that horse as a bucking horse. I don't think he had trouble with the horse, but he was worried for me because I was a green rider.

Dave had hired a number of men and slept with them in the bunkhouse. The cook, Mary Grant, lived in the house, which had a kitchen, a living room and two small bedrooms. In the winter, Mary went to live with her husband while Dave lived with one hired man in the house. There was no indoor plumbing. When I visited on weekends, I had some trouble with the cold wooden seat of the outdoor toilet.

I moved to Edmonton for the summer of '62 because I was attending summer school at the university. Early in July, Dave came up for the weekend. I don't think we even noticed the rain, but back home at Brownfield and Coronation it rained eight inches. The Battle River was so high that debris was caught 10 feet up in the willows that grew along the banks. People exchange stories even now of the flood of July 1962. When I was living on the acreage in the '80s, we discovered a ditch at the south edge of the property. The barnyard had been threatened by the flood waters, and so neighbours had dug the ditch to drain the yard.

That year, when I was teaching in Edmonton and travelling back and forth on the bus, Dave and I were getting to know each other and having our differences. He wanted me to leave my job, but I was committed to finishing my contract. I broke off our relationship at New Year's. Dave wasn't sure he wanted to take me back when I changed my mind.

Our Wedding

Dave and I planned to marry in July, as soon as my year at Mill Creek School in Edmonton was over, and so we began making preparations. I hadn't been very considerate of my young students when I made this decision. They would have to get used to a new teacher, as they didn't move on to the next grade like the others. My students varied in age from 8 to 12. I prepared coursework ranging from beginning reading to Grade 4 skills. I had to repeat and review materials, as the students didn't progress as quickly as the materials were organized. Some of my students acted out, so they were sent to see a psychologist. One of the youngest boys was still dealing with missing his previous teacher.

I didn't think that I should shop for a wedding dress if I didn't have an engagement ring, so Dave and I bought one at Camrose. My sisters both married soon after finishing university, so they wore short dresses at their marriage ceremonies. I had been working three years, so I bought a long dress. It had short sleeves. I had to have something borrowed for my wedding day, too. A woman I met on the bus loaned me her sheer fingerless gloves. I won't say what I wore that was blue.

I chose my sister Joan and Dave's sister Doris as my bridesmaids. I remember that we bought the turquoise fabric for the dresses, but I'm not sure who sewed them. An Edmonton seamstress sewed my turquoise wool boucle going-away skirt and jacket. I stood for a few fittings to make sure it fit me just right.

One weekend when I was at the ranch, I mixed and baked our wedding cake. Mary told me the oven was hotter than the gauge indicated. I also sewed a flowered dress I would wear for my bridal shower. The cake was inside the house the next week when an electrical fire started in the kitchen. The men got a rope around the deep-freeze and pulled it out of the burning building. Mary had thrown my cake out the window before the fire reached it, but many of her belongings were burned.

Now a new ranch house had to be built. I already had a book of Nelson precut homes, from which we chose a three-bedroom house with a laundry on the main floor. We needed a big kitchen and dining table because I made meals for the hired men. Sometimes there would be even more men when they rounded up the cattle for branding and vaccinating. We found that we needed to move the laundry down to the basement to make space. We also took a foot of space from the living room. I wanted an opening to the living room so I could see and talk to anyone in the other room while I was working in the kitchen.

On another weekend I was at our farm at Fleet. Grampa was going to miss my wedding because he was going to Ireland for the first time in 62 years. Mom and I drove him to the Fleet corner so he could catch the bus to Edmonton.

One of the men Dave chose to stand up with him at the altar left the area in order to avoid taking part in our wedding. I think he didn't like weddings, so we didn't take it personally. We were married in Fleet Church.

It wasn't large enough to accommodate a big wedding party, as some of the couples who were married in later years. Joan had married two years earlier; as I mentioned earlier, Julia and I had been her bridesmaids. Julia was married in Calgary in September of that same year, 1963.

The house was going up while we planned our wedding. Dave wanted to build a dropped entry at the back door so the men could take off their boots before coming inside. He had helped plan his mother's house, so some of his ideas for ours came from his experience with Allan and Irene's home. This turned out to be a good idea because we put a bathroom with a shower in the basement so the men could wash up before meals.

We advertised our wedding for Tuesday, July 2, 1963, with an open reception at the Fleet Hall to follow. We welcomed neighbours and friends from Fleet, Brownfield and Hardisty. Our dance was held in the Brownfield School gym. I enjoyed the music provided by the Storbakkens of Sedgewick because it sounded like the music played when I was learning to dance. Ian MacRae surprised us by paying for the band. His mother and Dave's mother had been very good friends when Ian and Dave were growing up. Ian was single at the time of our wedding, but he married soon thereafter.

Dave enjoyed visiting Jack and Mary MacRae. Mary had been such a good friend to his mother. When Jack was in hospital and slipped into a coma, Ian was with his mother when she cried out, "I can't live without my Jack." She had a heart attack and died. The family waited as

Jack slipped away. The two were buried together. I was amazed that they had such deep love for one another.

After we were married, we were late getting away from the reception dance. The last thing we did was help Daddy get into the truck so Mom could drive home. Since the Stettler Stampede was happening in town, we couldn't get a room, so we stayed in the honeymoon suite at the Halkirk Hotel.

We went to Buffalo Lake and Banff and to Lake Louise for our honeymoon. On our way home, we got to Calgary in time for the stampede parade. We saw the infield events and the chuck wagon races. It was dark when we went on the Wild Mouse ride, which took us on a high track at a fast rate of speed and then jerked us around sharp corners.

I was very tired as we headed home. Dave was driving on roads that were strange to me. I thought we were lost. I was trying to sleep. It was almost morning when we finally stopped at Drumheller for some sleep. When we got to the ranch, Mary, the cook, had all her belongings packed. She was ready to leave with her husband, Charlie, in his truck.

The new house wasn't finished, so Dave and I lived in the bunkhouse. I don't recall where the hired men slept, but we slept on a cot. We had the table and stove where I cooked and served meals to carpenters and the hired hands. When I found out the carpenters were sleeping on my new mattress in what would be our bedroom, I decided it was time for us to use our own furniture. The kitchen wasn't ready, so I still cooked the meals in the bunkhouse.

Dave had a dog called Nip. If he dropped a glove, Nip would pick it up in her teeth, put her foot on the stirrup and reach up with her mouth so Dave could take the glove. She would bite through a rope if you put it in her mouth.

Dave always took time to curry and work with his horses before he saddled them. If we were driving through the country, he would slow down the truck so he could get a better look at a horse out in the field. He went to horse auctions in Stettler. He would see the same horse again in a different field or else back at the auction. He wasn't surprised when an unsuitable, hard-to-handle horse was brought back and resold. When he looked at a horse, he was hoping to find evidence of good breeding. He would pay attention to body shape and to the neck and head. I tried to learn how to recognize a good horse, too.

We expected our first baby in June 1964. One evening, from the kitchen window of our new home, I watched a first calf heifer restlessly get up, lie down and rise again. Later I saw that she had given birth to her own calf. My mother died when I was young. I hadn't been able to talk to Mom about childbirth, but my two sisters and I were born close together, so I was hopeful that I wouldn't have too much trouble. Dave stayed with me all through the night. He rubbed my back and helped me through that frightening experience. He was on the way home to feed the hired men and start their day when Colin was born around 7:00 on a June morning.

Dave was out in the fields checking his cattle when he picked an armful of wild tiger lilies. They made a beautiful bouquet when we put them in a vase in my hospital room. I was overwhelmed by their beauty and the gesture of kindness from my shy husband. In those days, husbands were not invited into the delivery room. Dave was never even in the hospital when my babies were born. He may have been avoiding strong feelings or tempering his concern for me.

A schoolgirl helped me with the babies and the cooking during the summer. When she went back to school, I did the work alone in September. I would be quite tired at the end of a day, so I sat down to see that month's new television shows. After that point, I knew the characters, so I could listen to the programs while I did work in the kitchen. I was used to radio entertainment, so I didn't need to watch the images on the screen to have a fulfilling experience.

I was eight months' pregnant the first time I tried to get my driver's licence. We borrowed Doug Drever's car. I think it was a standard. I didn't have much experience driving. When I was younger and Daddy asked if I wanted to drive the tractor, I waited to be coaxed. Joan said, "I will." And off she went. Any time something was needed, she did it. I was nervous about my test. I made jerking starts and hesitant stops. I hoped the test administer would feel sorry for me, but I didn't pass. The next time I tried was after Colin was born. It was then that I got my driver's licence.

My former school superintendent, Jack Reid, came to the ranch in the second September after I was married. It was noon, all the ranch hands had come in for a meal, and my new baby, Colin, was crying because he was hungry and wanted breast milk. Mr. Reid never got around to asking me if I could teach.

A little later that fall, I discovered I was pregnant with our second child. Now I understood why my sister was born 11 months after I was.

Eunice Livingston helped me during the summer when Lee was expected and born. Her family lived across the river in a community called Battle Bend. She later went to Lamont for nursing training. My cousin Laverne and his wife were married the week before Lee was born. I made a lovely pink two-piece maternity outfit for the wedding. Lee was so tiny. l was too big to wear that outfit the next time I got pregnant.

Somehow, I was able and willing to have all my relatives come to the ranch the day after that wedding. I know the dessert was a raspberry cream pie, but I don't remember the rest of the meal.

When we brought Lee home from thc hospital, I looked to Colin to see if he was going to be jealous of his baby brother. The smiles I gave him helped him realize that we shared this new creature. The two babies were rarely apart. A photo of Lee always included Colin. I had two in cloth diapers and a wringer washing machine. The diaper fabric was just thin enough that it loved to wrap around the wringers that squeezed the water out of the diapers before I could rinse them and hang them on the line to dry.

Automatic washers and dryers were coming into vogue. Farm wives often had to do without modern conveniences because purchasing farm machinery was more important, as it was necessary to earn money for the family. There was one advocate of automatic washers and dryers in our community. She grew up in another part of the province and wasn't afraid to say what she thought. She raved about the new laundry equipment. You didn't even have to iron the shirts after they came out of the dryer, she told me. I did get a new top-loading washer and dryer, and I have her and my two babies to thank.

Colin, Leland and Kelly were all born at Castor Hospital. Leland was born July 1965 at lunchtime. Kelly arrived April 1968 at suppertime. Kelly came so fast that the doctor wasn't there when he was born. Sister Barnard was a capable midwife. When I saw that my third son had more of my father's looks, I found him an Irish name. It seemed that Kelly started running as soon as he could walk. He was always trying to keep up with his brothers.

When Dr. Foster left Castor Hospital, I went to Coronation to have Tyler. He was due at Christmas but showed up just in time to be the New Year's baby: January 2, 1972.

The Hardisty Stampede was the biggest event in our calendar year. Dave's sport was rodeo. He talked about team roping before I even knew what it was. Our sons were pulling on cowboy boots and playing with ropes as soon as they could walk. One evening, Dave was sleeping on the couch. The boys put a rope around his ankle and tied him to the doorknob. When Lee was barely big enough to get on the spring horse, he rode it so hard that we weren't sure if it would last long enough for Kelly to ride it, too.

I was outside talking while Dave held the reins of his saddled horse. Lee asked if he could ride with his dad, and Dave said no. While we weren't paying attention, Lee pulled himself up onto that full-size horse and into the saddle. He did get to ride after all.

Sometime after that, we were able to acquire smaller horses for the boys to ride. Silver was a white Shetland with some splashes of black. Penny was so small that one might have thought her to be a toy. The kids would sit on her when she was lying down.

In 1969, Ken and Dave sold half the cattle and divided Crystal Springs Ranch into two parcels—so Dave had fewer cattle, less land and fewer hired men to manage. Ken rented out his half, so it was available when his son Dale was ready to farm. As boys, Dale, Colin and Lee would play at ranching, and they all grew up to be ranchers.

Dogs were always an important part of farm life. We had Dixie on our farm when I was growing up, and Dave had his dog, Nip. Sometimes we would try to find another dog. Sometimes it wouldn't be suitable and we would take it back to its owner. One time we had a pup that was later run over in the yard.

I'm not sure which dog was Lee's best buddy. Lee had a brown bear coat like the one I had as a little girl. He was wearing it out in the yard, maybe when Colin was already going to school. He was romping with this dog across the dry winter grass. If Lee or the dog got hurt, they would separate and glare at each other. In no time, they would be back rolling over and over on the ground.

My father was a careful driver. He always started braking well before he came to a corner or stop. One day he drove Mom and my three brothers to the ranch for a visit. I was surprised when I looked out the window and saw them driving into the yard with his dog riding on all four feet on the cab of the truck. That dog had been there for 36 miles from the farm near Fleet to the ranch.

In March 1971 we celebrated 25 years of my parents' marriage at the Fleet Hall. My sisters came with husbands and families. I made a speech about our family experiences. Eddy English had some interesting recollections that he shared while threatening to take his notes out of his pocket.

After 10 years and four sons, we decided to move off the ranch, with its grain farming and grain dust, to set up on a different ranch in British Columbia. This was a natural progression for me. My grandfather had moved to B.C. when I was 10. I had learned to swim there when I was 18. My sister Julia and her husband were living in Osoyoos. We were looking forward to more family time.

The Baptist minister from Fairfield was the school bus driver who discovered Dave's accident when he came through on a day when Brownfield students didn't have to attend classes. I had my housecoat on when I went to the bus to tell the minister that the elementary students didn't have school that day. Minutes later, he was back. He said that something had happened to Dave. I put on my coat and grabbed a blanket.

We found Dave lying on the road beside his truck. His face was so white. His coat had opened up. I looked at the green shirt on his chest. There was a small hole in it, and there was blood around the hole. I didn't check for a pulse.

Reverend Reitan and Dave's faithful dog stayed until the police and ambulance came. I made arrangements for Joe Richardson to take my children to his home. By this time, Brownfield High School students were going to Coronation. They were waiting for the bus and soon learned that a terrible tragedy had happened. It was very hard for me to tell my own children that their father was dead. I tried to put it off.

I'm reminded of that morning and of the morning I saw the white sheet on top of Dr. Cousineau's car. I read the new Castor history *Beaver Tales* and found this: "Doc often went with the funeral director to pick up a deceased person."

Family members had arrived while the police were investigating. They didn't want me to get in the car with the police. I knew the routine. I didn't know what they would ask me. They told me that my husband's death was an accident.

The police didn't ask me any questions, but I had plenty of my own.

Dave's brothers and sisters came to the house as we prepared for the funeral and shared our loss. People brought food from as far away as Wetaskiwin. Bouquets of flowers filled the house. At one point, I brought out my photo albums to affirm that I would keep wonderful memories. I was saddened to see Dave's oldest brother so bereft as he walked out in the yard. He had been seriously injured when a grain truck had run over him, but he had survived. Donald had been hurt. Allan had lost an eye. I thought the family was invincible.

I also thought that I could handle death better than this loving, caring family could. I didn't cry at the funeral. I was still in shock, but I did feel the caring concern of all who came to share our grief. Dave was known, loved and appreciated for his friendliness and good humour. He liked to greet each person by his or her first name.

Questions

The questions I had when Dave died have hung around, and they surface at any time—for example, the time when my grandson was in the local tire shop. I'm glad he came to me. I felt deep sadness as I mulled over the conversation I had had with Luke. Someone had told him that his grandfather had killed himself. I mentioned this to my sister, who has a low tolerance for negativity. She said that that was a lie. "You have to stop that one in its tracks," she said. Outright denial doesn't allow the background of my story to emerge, however. My sister has little patience for my truth.

Yes, it had been calving time when my husband had died. He'd been treating the livestock for scours that morning. He hated coyotes hanging around at calving time, as he didn't want them chewing on a newborn calf that hadn't yet stood for the first time. Maybe he was careless with the gun when his stomach growled as he digested the leftover salmon sandwiches I gave him for breakfast. We celebrated Kelly's fifth birthday on Monday. This was Tuesday.

A sudden death, especially one delivered from the barrel of a gun, is suspicious. Dave's gun wasn't supposed to be loaded. It had a clip to hold the bullets. It could be stored separately from the ammunition. People talk, though. They make up their own minds. One family said it was my idea to move to B.C., that Dave hadn't wanted to relocate. I had my own history with suicide, and Dave had his. In our community, some deaths seemed obviously to be gunshot suicides. Maybe one story about a woman from Alliance who allegedly killed herself was fabricated. She had the doctors' book out to find out where her heart was located in her chest. Did she kill herself with a .22 rifle?

We had all heard stories of people living for years with mental illness and finally deciding to end their lives. I was in Calgary after two of my husbands died. I couldn't find a parking spot on a Sunday. I wanted to go to a 12-step breakfast meeting. I went to Chapters instead and there found the Miriam Toews book *Swing Low: A Life.* A title like that got my attention. The book was about her father. He was a wonderful teacher who spent his weekends in bed with deep depression. He lived so many years with mental illness and one day walked in front of a train to end his life.

I have to be truthful. The hurt that smoulders inside me has to come out. I am angry because people have refused to hear and understand me. The flame will burst forth. The hurt I've experienced will fall on these pages. When Dave died suddenly, I was shocked. I thought that we were finishing a chapter in his life, but now it was the end of the book. While I try to protect all the people I love, I simply have to write out my pain, all the stories I've held inside.

I remember a day when I was getting ready to drive to Coronation for a hair appointment. Dave came to me. "You have to listen to me. Gottlieb [our hired man] can see the pain I'm in. He knows how bad I feel. It's too much for me. I feel so down."

I had been so busy with our fourth child. I was busy being a mother. I wasn't aware of the mental struggle Dave had been undergoing—since January, perhaps, and now it was May.

I'd been taking the baby with me to community meetings.
Two consultants had come to our rural area to lead Man
and Resources meetings. It felt good to be seen as a leader.
As country people, we were glad to be consulted. Rural
communities were facing changes. Later, in Edmonton,
I became interested in a course called Community
Development. It helped me understand what the Institute
of Man and Resources was trying to do. I had been
chosen to attend a national conference in Toronto.

Dave had made bargains with God. For example, he said,
"I won't kill myself if . . ." We went to see counsellors and
a psychiatrist. He took pills but didn't like the taste in
his mouth.

One counsellor asked me how important the upcoming
trip to Toronto was to me. I got the idea that he was
saying that Dave's illness was my fault. I cancelled my
trip, and a friend went in my place.

I had had visions and dreams of watching our boys grow
up on our ranch by the Battle River. I could see our
family growing and succeeding there, but Dave decided
that we would sell it and move to B.C. The grain dust
bothered him. On more than one occasion in spring, he
had gone to Uncle Kenny about leaving or selling. He
wasn't feeling the optimism one needs for spring seeding.
He was 43; he might have been having a midlife crisis.
We were making trips to B.C. and looking at cow–calf
operations there.

When my husband died suddenly, seemingly by his own
hand, I was left with many questions and many things

to think about. Did he want this? There had been times when he and his brothers had been careless about their own safety. In the winter, for example, Dave took us on a wild ride on the Ski-Doo. We bounced over the swales of the former oxbows and landed on the frozen water. I knew he had thought about suicide when he was in the depths of his depression.

I thought, though, that he had a new lease on life. He made a plan to take his little family and start over in B.C. He wanted to concentrate on the cattle ranching that he loved. He would be able to handle the cattle on horseback with his sons riding beside him. He had already sold the ranch to our nephew. The cattle we had trailed in from the hills behind a pickup load of feed on March 12 were no longer ours. The calves Dave had treated for scours that morning weren't his anymore, either.

He hadn't found the ranch that was supposed to be our new home. When he went to Lytton after a flight into Kamloops, he learned that the irrigation pipes required too much handling to grow the hay that would sustain the cattle over the winter months. British Columbian ranches usually included forest grazing, so cattle spent the summers eating under the trees. It might be hard to find and check them, he thought.

Money was accumulating as we were finalizing the sale of our assets. On one occasion, my husband asked me, "How much money do we have now?" Maybe he thought we wouldn't have enough to buy in at B.C.

Revelations

The confusion I felt after my husband died so suddenly led me to make connections between my father's experiences and my own. I read the book of Revelation and saw that John and David, the respective names of my father and husband, are included along with ideas of Easter death and the Second Coming. The book of Revelation also features the number seven.

I associated Dave's birthday of June 7 with his death on April 17, 1973, and these I linked with my previous belief that the Second Coming would happen in the 1970s. The brand we put on our cattle was 711. A game Dave liked to play at the midway, during the stampedes, was Seven Over, Seven Under. He participated in no other gambling. While quite capable of picking a horse that would win at the horse races, he refused to place any bets.

I tried to make sense of his death using my childlike faith. Dave died at the beginning of the Easter holidays, on the Tuesday before Good Friday. We usually thought a funeral should take place three days after a person's death. I thought that he would be buried on Good Friday. No one wanted that to happen, so we held his funeral on Holy Saturday.

I had a sense that Christ was with us. I was in shock and I was numb, but the light of the spring day seemed so bright. I was turned around in my tracks, glad that it was spring because I could look ahead to the better weather and new beginnings.

After my husband died on April 17, 1973, my aunt told me that my mother had died on April 17 in 1946. I thought that this coincidence had special meaning.

Dave had yearned for the softness of a daughter. He didn't bounce two little girls in blue on his knee like my grandfather did. I phoned from the hospital to tell him that our fourth child was another boy. His voice had a catch in it that communicated his disappointment. It wasn't until then that I knew he hankered for a baby girl as much as I did. His sadness came on so soon. I learned that men can suffer from postpartum depression. I didn't know about this condition until I worked with and helped widows at Calgary Family Services. The postpartum section was in the rooms across the hall from us.

My mother was stricken immediately after my youngest sister was born. I blame my father's drinking and her father's religion. I can also say that having three little girls born so close together contributed to her mental breakdown. Baby blues were not recognized at that time.

My sister Joan has provided me with telling insights over the years. When our children were babies, we were discussing our mother's nervous breakdown. She said that at the time, Mom's difficulty would have been noted and that help might have been available. I still don't think it was a good thing for the parties who made the decision to take our mother away from us. I don't think it was good for her, either. Our rural area still urgently needs better mental health information and services.

It is so hard to write stories of my husband who died. It is hard to write about the happy times. When I write down the good times, I feel sad because I am reminded of how much I lost. Soon after Dave died, I had a dream. We were on a beautiful road somewhere in B.C. He gave me a team of horses. I was supposed to hold their reins at their heads. He left me holding the reins. In another dream, I put my head on his shoulder and nestled my face into his neck. I thought he might not like my cold nose touching his bare neck.

When I think about losing Dave, it resurrects my feelings of not being good enough. I thought I was being punished by God when Dave died. I didn't cry at the funeral, but I cried every time I went to church. When I opened up my throat to sing the songs I loved, the feelings came. I couldn't hold them back. I stopped attending services. I lost sight of Jesus' love. I'm not sure I ever felt or understood love. All of the critical, judgmental stuff from the past flared up in my face after I lost my first husband.

Strict religious lessons haunted me when I found myself single again in the seventies. The people who attended the Baptist church were more like the fanatical religious people I had turned against as a young person. I thought that I shouldn't date until a year had passed.

I returned to Naramata for family camp with my sons. My father was able to help me during this difficult time. He told me that the Elks were having a convention in Penticton that summer. He drove us with the tent trailer so we could camp at Naramata. Each day he made the trip to Penticton to attend his convention.

My father also had a new school bus that needed to be driven all the way across Canada. By this time, Uncle Willie was at Owen Sound, Ontario, and his oldest son, David, was in a high-rise apartment in Toronto. When we visited him, we could see a lot of the city from his balcony.

Dave had an aunt named Doris in Windsor, Ontario. I took Kelly and Lee to visit her while we waited for Daddy to bring Colin. We worked in some visits with Wideman relatives, too. They lived in a rural area, but the houses and farms were so close together that my sons wondered how there was room for farming. I was able to take a photo of the Wideman stone house where my grandfather grew up.

Then it was time to go to Brantford to pick up the bus and set out on the trip home. I, my three oldest sons, and my dad slept each night on the floor of the bus. I had been the navigator for Dave when we drove in the city, so I was able to direct Daddy through the Ontario cities. I was glad I didn't have to drive. For me and the boys, it was really hard to pass by all those Ontario lakes without even walking out onto the beach. We saw Niagara Falls from a distance. There was a waterwheel at Owen Sound, and I realized that my father was afraid of the water, especially when my sons were involved.

Each morning we would wake at 5:00 and drive all day until 10:00 p.m. In two and a half days, we were home in Alberta. Tyler stayed at the farm with Hazel.

In September, my sons went to school with the Bedson family so I could return by plane to Naramata to attend

Transactional Analysis with Muriel and John James. I needed these workshops to try to find out how to deal with the changes I had to endure in my young life.

The first night I cried when we sang "Home on the Range" while sitting around the piano. "Oh, give me a home . . . where the deer and antelope play." My home on the range was never again going to be what it had once been.

Our facilitators spoke to the whole group, and then we broke off into smaller groups where United Church ministers led our discussions. I heard many ideas that were new to me. I was learning how our experiences in life influence our reactions. I was vulnerable because I was still grieving my husband's death. When I had and shared a new insight, I thought I was providing help for others as well as for myself.

My group leader was getting on the same plane as I. I thought of him as a sky pilot. He offered me a Life Saver and I thought, *Am I saved?* It took me back to the evangelical meetings of my childhood.

A new song was playing on the radio. At first, I thought the song referred to one of the other attendees. It took me a while to see that it told my story. "She walks downtown with a suitcase in her hand," wearing "a faded rose from days gone by." I was *Delta Dawn*. The rose was the yellow rose from my wedding bouquet and the yellow roses I had requested for Dave's casket. "A mysterious dark-haired man" will "take [her] to his mansion in the sky." When I got back to Edmonton, my driver, who was my special friend, was waiting for me at the other airport.

I had to have him paged so he could come pick me up from the downtown airport.

My behaviour seemed bizarre. Reverend and Mrs. Reitan stayed with me one night. I saw judgment in her pursed lips. I hadn't gotten my kids from the Bedsons' place yet. My husband's family and my father decided that I needed to be taken to Alberta Hospital Ponoka. My dad took on that job, so I rode with him and his friend Eddie English. They made sure I was comfortable for the drive. Some of the time, I was sitting in the front of the car.

Daddy took me into the facility and up to the registration desk. I had been sitting with the man in charge for a few short moments before he decided that I didn't belong there. Dad was already back at the car. I ran out to the parking lot to stop him before he left.

I stayed at the farm with my parents and my brothers for a few days to recover from my emotional emergency. It took me many years to process what happened, though. So many thoughts were swirling in my mind. I also had a clarity that I couldn't explain to anyone I knew at the time. I would later learn the designation *spiritual emergency,* which seems to describe my experience best.

Our First Year without Dave

We stayed on the ranch for a year. Chickenpox had been circulating among Brownfield students since February, but my boys hadn't gotten sick. Now it was April. Two weeks after their father died, my kids got chickenpox.

They brought it home to Tyler. He was so sick that I held him and rocked him all night. In the next two years, the kids would contract measles and mumps.

George, who loved children, was born to Maori parents while they worked in the pineapple fields of Hawaii. He came to Coronation as a farm worker. He worked on the ranch for a few years before operating the packer tractor for the county. He often visited on weekends and helped with gardening and childcare. He had a great sense of loyalty to his former boss, Dave, and had grave concern for my sons. Just weeks after our loss, George brought a mountain ash tree for Mother's Day. He had the boys help him plant the tree that still shades the cement patio where my oldest son, his wife and their adult sons live.

Dave hadn't had the opportunity to see Tyler ride a horse and enjoy it. That spring after Dave died, when the weather warmed up, the boys started him riding Penny— and soon he was the fourth little cowboy. Sometimes Lee would be an Indian with a feather in his headband and fringes on his vest.

One day the boys were washing dishes at the kitchen sink. Lee was shirtless, standing on a turquoise chair with his hands in the sink. His blue jeans rested on his hips, exposing the elastic of his underwear. Tyler, with elbows on the counter, stood on the same chair. The strap of his red overalls had hitched up his T-shirt in the back. Colin faced Lee with an orange-bordered tea towel. His sleeves were rolled up, and his toes touched another chair as he lounged on the counter. Kelly, also shirtless, sat on the counter and received the dried dishes.

Dave had done most of the driving when he was alive. If he was tired, then I would help him. His foot would relax on the gas pedal as he headed for a ditch. I would catch him and wake him.

One night when there was still a lot of snow, Dave and I were driving home from the rodeo held each spring at the Edmonton Coliseum. We had all the kids in the back. I would have liked to stay overnight in a hotel. I drove from Edmonton to Daysland. Then Dave took over. At Killam, he bought coffee to stay awake. I decided I could go to sleep. We landed in the snow-filled ditch before we made it to Lougheed. The mail truck pulled us out. Ours were the only vehicles on the road that late at night.

Now I was doing all the driving. We didn't have seat belts or child car seats or booster seats. If I hit the brakes, I would automatically reach out my right arm to restrain the child next to me. And while Dave had been the one to squirt gas (*squirt* was the word he used) into our vehicles, now it was my job. Once I began driving all the time, I often forgot to look at the gas gauge. On three occasions, I ran out of gas. It was usually around our neighbourhood, so someone would help me.

My car was a Pontiac Parisienne. It was a big blue boat that once went into the ditch when I got a flat tire. That was when Dave was still alive. I had been carrying a carload of root pickers from Coronation when the tire went flat. I couldn't control the Parisienne. Soon enough, Dave, too, would find that the car handled differently than did the trucks that he was used to driving.

I wasn't experienced with every kind of road condition and was maybe a little overconfident and distracted when I had begun driving all the time. I would slip into the ditch when there was mud, ice or heavy snow. Once, when I was turning into Coronation while the road was icing, I hit the ditch. They were building a new road through the ravine close to the Bedsons'. My car left the road and landed down the slope, making it almost to the trees. My groceries were scattered all over the inside of the vehicle. Jim had to pull me out with the tractor. My problem wasn't having collisions; it was going into the ditch.

Another time I was driving when the boys asked if Tyler, who was a year and a half, could have a candy. The next thing I knew, he was choking. I had to stop the car. The candy came out, but my car was high-centred on the edge of the ditch. We had to walk down the road, all five of us, to get help. Another time, we walked when the motor quit and I had no idea what was wrong. I hope we would have stayed with the car if it had been wintertime.

I also let my driver's licence lapse. I had forgotten to renew it for so many months that I had to do another driving test. I asked Marie to drive me to Stettler for the test. I was nervous again this time, but I passed.

Bankers Row

I was hoping to find acreage and build a new house. Dave's estate wasn't settled, so I didn't have much money. Our nephew and his new wife were living in a mobile home on the ranch and would soon move into the house. I found a home that a senior couple was selling. They had moved into Castor from the farm and hadn't done any repairs on the old home. I bought it for $10,000.

When I moved with my sons to this two-storey house, there was room for George, as well. The interior included two fireplaces and had window seats positioned below the leaded windows. There was a fir-panelled room we used as a dining room. The ceilings were nine feet high. I decided that I needed a chime clock for this room. That way, we wouldn't have to move from room to room to know what time it was. I bought the chime clock on one of my trips to Edmonton.

The house was built in the 1920s when the wealthier people of the town settled the street that soon became known as Bankers Row. This house was the Rombough house when I lived in Castor with my mother, and there are two photos of it in the new Castor history: *Beaver Tales*.

One of our first projects was to remove the lilacs that had obliterated the walkway in front of the old house. George and I used an axe to chop out the tangled roots that had grown over and under the cement sidewalk.

There was asparagus and horseradish on the property, which had been moved to new patches when they became overgrown. They, however, hadn't tackled the spreading lilacs. We planted some junipers inside the newly revealed sidewalk.

There was a long driveway along the south side of the house. It reached the backyard and garden. The house had a back door with a raised outdoor landing.

We stayed in Castor for two years. My youngest child wasn't in school yet. The other three attended school in the same building where I had gone to high school. One of my old classmates was a teacher to one of them. When I would go out at night with some of my friends, George was there for the boys.

I earned a teaching certificate that had required two years of university education. I was able to attend one course at Hanna on Saturdays and another at Killam on Wednesday nights. I was working toward getting my bachelor of education degree.

The boys played hockey and rode their bikes. One day they were outside when it started to rain. I looked out and saw one of my friends taking their bikes out of his van. My friends were the young single people in the community.

I liked to go to the Cosmopolitan Hotel bar on Thursday nights and Saturday afternoon. One such occasion took place on the night before my substitute assignment at the high school. I started asking around and found one of the high school students. I hoped they would take it easy on me the next day.

My father also liked to frequent the bar, so it wasn't long before gossip about me reached his ears. He came to see me to express his concern. He knew and I knew that I was old enough to manage my own affairs.

Around this time, I met Leslie and Brian, who were preparing and printing the *Castor Advance*. One day Leslie told me that she was going to a meeting in Stettler. I found out that Grant Notley was going to be there at the meeting of the Alberta New Democrats. Leslie didn't think I would be interested. The party was looking for people to let their names stand for election to the Alberta Legislature. Grant asked me to be a candidate for Sedgewick–Coronation. The election took place in 1975.

I knew the party's philosophy from my university days, when I had experience with the Christian Student Movement and the CCF. I attended New Democratic Party (NDP) conventions to familiarize myself with current policies, and there I enjoyed talking with older members of the party. I felt passionate about the plans we made for improving the lives of farmers and workers. I wanted people to feel less apathy about elections and government. I also wanted to instill in them the confidence that they could effect change and improve their lives.

I enjoyed visiting communities that supported the Cooperative Movement and the old CCF party. I enjoyed meeting people and listening to their ideas. I was able to organize and deliver speeches. It was fun to be in parades, holding my sign and waving to all the families gathered in the small towns.

My party supported women as candidates. I encouraged women to be more independent and so was troubled when women told me that they had voted for whom their husbands did. I was also disturbed when people thought that only men should be in government.

My sons and I were learning to ski at the Valley Ski Club on the Battle River north of Castor. My sister Joan was living in Dallas, Texas, so she gave me her family's ski equipment. I took the three oldest boys to Disney World. Joan and Zahid and their three boys met us there. They were camping.

I still had the blue Pontiac. I filled it up before I left and accidentally left my credit card at the gas station. Once I arrived in Florida, I realized I didn't have it on me. I had to send back to my bank for money.

One of the Hallet girls, all of whom were older than I, stayed on her parents' farm when they went to Russia on a trip. I got to know her and her family that summer when I was home from university. We kept in touch after that. In the seventies she divorced, so she started Day Five, which was a club for singles in Edmonton. I would drive to Edmonton for Friday night parties held in members' homes.

I ordered a brand new, two-tone Buick Century. It was red and tan. I went to Stettler to pick it up on the first day new cars were being sold that year. At Christmas, I was disappointed when I hit the ditch with my new car. The boys and I were driving to have Christmas at Martin and Esther's when it happened.

I had driven on the highway to Coronation and was going north on the Brownfield Road, which was paved by that time. I came over a hill and saw two cars, side by side, ahead of me. I hit the brakes and flew into the ditch. I had no idea that the road was covered in glare ice. I floated all the way to the fence in the soft snow. The people in those cars had not stopped. They were meeting each other, but I hadn't had time to assess the situation. Eventually a truck came along and pulled us out. A piece of moulding was torn off the side of the car. My previous ditch-driving mishaps hadn't damaged my car, but this one had.

We Move to Edmonton

I bought a house and moved to Edmonton. Tyler was ready for kindergarten, and my other boys were old enough to look after each other while I went to night classes at university. I was taking French. It would help me build a future in politics, I figured. I put poor little

Tyler into French immersion class. His brothers teased him for it, and he didn't do very well in school. He had to take a second year of kindergarten. I was already registered for day classes. I found a neighbour down the street whose boy was in Tyler's class. They played together in the afternoons.

While we were living in Edmonton, I wanted to recognize the fact that we were a family, so I arranged to have a family photo taken. We had an appointment for a sitting when the photographer phoned to reschedule because his studio wasn't yet completed. A few minutes after the call came in, Tyler decided to cut his hair with the scissors. He chopped into his bangs. That little incident is memorialized in our family photo—as it shall be for the rest of his life.

I was living in Edmonton with my sons when Helen Reddy sang me another song, "Gladiola." The line "Hear me, Gladiola, I can read your mind, it looks as though you've been crying for such a long time" spoke directly to me. How could Helen Reddy know that I was Gladys all those years ago when I went to school? I was nicknamed Gladiola Bulbs, or Bulbs for short.

On a dreary winter day, my French professor was not available for a promised tutoring session. I was having trouble learning this language, even though I had taken three years of French in high school. My psychology paper was not coming together, either. I was writing about my process of becoming aware. I was an adult with children. I felt disconnected from the younger students at university, who were just away from home and had no family duties.

I went to the student mall called The Hub. The main floor's food kiosks lined the three-storey hallway, with residences overlooking the action. I bought a piece of carrot cake with cream cheese icing and sat down to eat it when I heard loud noises. Snap! Crash! Bang! Pop! Pieces of glass fell into an ice cream pail.

The stain glass artist was working in a display he had set up in the mall. His works consisted of coloured glass soldered together into a design. There, I found some clear glass soldered together. "That was frost-cracked; interesting how it broke; I put it back together," he said. Another piece caught my eye: it was teardrop-shaped with a large bubble of amber glass and with a smaller, clear bubble near that one. The piece was intricate, just the right size to fit into the palm of my hand.

He said, "I designed that one when I was sitting in my doctor's office. I named it 'Verily, the Eye of Emptiness.'"

It hit a chord for me, so I said, "I'd like to buy that one."

"Oh, that one belongs to my roommate. I can make another one for you. It can be a reason to see you again."

This surprised me. I hadn't thought of him that way. He was young and very thin.

The next time I saw him, he was set up in the Social Sciences Building. "Could you bring me a cup of coffee?" He didn't want to leave his projects unattended. My item wasn't finished. He would call me, he said.

When the phone rang, I saw it was a rescue. My Easter date had promised a trip to the mountains. He arrived with an armload of liquor products instead. My holiday, when my sons had gone to their uncle's, was too important to spend with that clown. After I received the call from the stained glass artist, I announced to my date that he had to leave.

It was Saturday, and spring had reached the city streets. The fresh air was more intoxicating than sweet liqueur and bubbly wine. The artist invited me for a jog. He showed no embarrassment at being followed by an older woman who was unaccustomed to running in public. I struggled to keep up.

He confided, "If you are in poor health and rundown, wear a tracksuit to improve your image. Good for impressing women."

He talked about roommates in a co-op house. He had worked as an electrician installing lamps. When I visited his workshop in the basement of the "house," the leftover lamp chains hung as a curtain.

He talked about getting his act—or, as he called it, his shit—together. His roommates wanted him to do that, too. Listening to records in my basement, I touched the soft cotton cloth gathered at his shoulder. I felt his spare, hard body.

I requested a lamp, red and gold, for my bedroom. He did not believe his luck: he had sold a lamp! That was easy. Or was he selling himself? We went to the stained glass shop to pick out the bright glass for the lamp I had found in one of his books.

Soon he was set up in my city garage, snapping off the pieces of glass to make my lamp, plus a more elaborate one with flowers worked into it for a Vancouver customer.

After two years in the city, I needed one more course to complete my degree. The boys had been moping around our backyard, as they are country boys. The two older ones had their own roping horses. I was still getting the *Coronation Review* and saw that Allan Chinnery was advertising acreage for sale. It sounded interesting. When I talked to Allan, he told me that there was a creek. Remember that I had tried to find acreage after Dave died when the boys and I were leaving the farm.

Acreage Living

On a weekend, Bob (the stained glass artist), I and the boys went to check out the property. The boys were wandering around the yard and barn when I asked Bob where we would build the new house. I was thinking the northeast corner, which was sheltered on two sides by tall spruce and pine trees. His choice was the location of the older house previously owned by Stan and Edna Bullick. They had one daughter, so the house had two tiny bedrooms and one larger one. My boys were going to be crowded.

The house was white with clapboard siding and green trim. The roof was cottage-style, steep enough to have an attic. Huge pine trees stood in the front yard. There was a white picket fence that would soon need some repair. A garage was nestled in a poplar grove. The knoll on the west side of the acreage had three small wooden grain bins.

I was very clear that I wouldn't make the move without the help of a partner. How could I do all the things the acreage needed if I was alone with my four growing boys? Living out of town would also mean a certain amount of driving.

Soon we were packing up our things and preparing for the move.

In the summer of 1978, Bob and I moved my family to a 14-acre former farm site. We also rented 20 acres of pasture for Colin and Lee's team roping horses. Cows and Bantam chickens were added to the mix. I may have lost track of some of our animals, but I do know that the pigs lived long enough to celebrate their birthdays. They had gotten a disease that had stunted their growth.

My sons enjoyed helping their uncles and neighbours with cattle roundups. They spent many hours testing and developing their horses and their ranching skills. They were riding Silver one day, and the next day they found her with a new baby mule. The Shetland stayed at Richard Scheffelmaier's while we were living in the city so his donkey could impregnate the 13-year-old. She stayed after the first mule was born.

Lee had been home for about three weeks. He'd been quite sick. I think it might have been the beginning of his arthritis. The other boys went to school and phoned home. They told Lee to see what was wrong with Hairy Legs, his team roping horse. Lee was on a tear to see what the problem was. He found a new foal. The stallion would have been back at Duke Ranches. We had no idea that we had a second pregnant horse.

When my sons rode the school bus out of the yard and up the first hill, they could look to the Nose Hills off on their right. I often admired those hills. They would take on the colours of the season. I couldn't look too long, though, because someone might come flying over the crest of our little hill and crash into me. One time I was driving home and Bob surprised me. I drove into the ditch to avoid hitting him. I had a Toyota car, and he had a Toyota Land Cruiser.

There was the time I came home to find the truck badly mangled. The roof was smashed in, the windows broken. Bob was sleeping downstairs and looked a little banged up. He had been drinking and joyriding in the Nose Hills, and he had rolled the truck.

Bob and I established Ribstone Glass Art Ltd. He was a collector of building materials and old woodworking tools. We traded with the Coronation Senior Centre, exchanging a stained glass window for the old bricks of the telephone building. We got the metal ceiling tiles from Stubbs' store before it was torn down. We bought materials from Clark's Lumber, which was closing in Edmonton after 100 years in business.

The four-sided planer was a cast iron monster that only Bob would recognize. I think we found it halfway to Camrose. Hauling it to our acreage was another adventure. The process of getting it into production was a test. We didn't have enough electricity to make the four turning blades cut into the lumber. One of the Hutterites from the Veteran Colony tried a series of transformers, but that didn't work. We finally hooked it up to the power takeoff of a John Deere 4010 tractor, which was something my sons understood.

We produced tongue-and-groove panelling and many mouldings from fir, spruce and cedar. We also produced piles and piles of wood shavings, which we hauled to the Castor rodeo grounds that were being established on land my cousin had provided.

We took the horse trailer to a place outside Saskatoon where there were all kinds of hardwoods. The proprietor would buy green hardwood lumber from the States and bring it back to Canada. He had school buses on his property that acted as kilns in the dry prairie climate. We bought honey locust, black walnut and white oak boards. The hardwood was so heavy, it's a wonder we made it home. The axle bowed under the weight, so the tires were riding on their edges.

Bob and I married near Cumberland Head on Lake Champlain in upstate New York on September 14, 1980. This lake and Plattsburg were his home growing up.

Bob was born in Montreal. His family decided to move to Georgia. They didn't get that far, but some of their family members did move farther afield. When Bob and I got married, Jeff and Mary Kay were living in Atlanta. They stood up with us when we were wed.

On the Edge

One summer day in 1982, Bob left the farm in an agitated state. He said I couldn't go with him. I was worried and hoped he would be home soon. When he didn't come, I went to Castor to visit my friends. Cathy was milking her cows while I told her about our troubled relationship. She used a term I didn't understand: *hit bottom.* I'm not sure if she meant that I had hit bottom or that Bob had hit bottom. After supper, the subject of suicide came up, and I consciously pushed the idea away from my mind. I stayed overnight with Cathy. The rooster was crowing and the chickens were squawking when I slipped out of the house the next morning.

I drove home to our acreage. I couldn't find Bob. The dog, Zeke, walked along with me as I searched. I found the Toyota truck parked at the northwest corner of the property. I found a suicide note in the truck. I was very distressed as I tried to find Bob in one of our buildings. I looked under the pine trees and in the poplar groves.

I phoned the police to help me. I was terrified about what I would find. My neighbour had left a note that had more meaning for the police than it did for me. Allan had written it before he found Bob in an advanced state of intoxication and barely conscious. Bob had taken pills and alcohol, and Allan took him to hospital. I went there to see him. I didn't want to take him home. I thought he needed more help than I could give him.

Bob was still hallucinating from the effects of the drugs, but he insisted that I take him home. I was still in shock when we began attending 12-step recovery programs in the basement of the United Church.

I watch television when there is a show that touches on my own experience. I turn to watch when I hear about Sid Vicious of Sex Pistols fame. When I see him dance to live up to his name, I am reminded of Bob's dance, which I could not understand, relate to or dance along with. It consisted of wild jumping up and down. I recall hearing Bob mention Sid Vicious. Hard rock wasn't of much interest to my country boys. In the 1980s, music videos were particularly absorbing for Bob. We all sat down and watched because they were new on television.

Sid Vicious died around the time I met Bob. Drug-induced deaths had a way of getting our attention. John Belushi died when we were at the acreage. After Bob died, I read the book Bob Woodward had written about John, as well as the one John's widow wrote.

I try to understand these characters who resembled Bob. When I was living at Castor with my sons, I was fascinated with Janis Joplin and her music. I was reading *Buried Alive,* the book about her life. I was even drinking Southern Comfort, her drink. I was interested to read about her life, which seemed to have no limits. She appeared to give too much of herself. I try to understand why fame and music and all that surrounds it can lead to death. Elvis Presley was another one who died of an apparent overdose.

I could see the similarities between Janis and Bob: drugs, music, art, creativity, no limits. I listened to Janis sing "Piece of My Heart" and saw her performance style on television. She put everything into it. She didn't keep anything back for herself. This last is where I share things in common with her: no boundaries, generous to a fault, giving myself away, needing to be needed, meeting others' needs before they even have time to ask. I was not able or willing to see that harm could come to me and my family.

I went headlong into my marriage with enthusiasm and energy, trusting that I wouldn't get hurt. I did get hurt. It has taken me a long time to grasp the progressive nature of addiction. The addict needs more and more of his or her drug to get the desired effect. The body builds a resistance to the substance. If the drinking or drug-using behaviour is distressing to the spouse, then things will only get worse.

Bob knew he had some elements of bipolar disorder. He talked to his mother about lithium. He didn't want to take it. He thought it would dampen his creativity. He had started using drugs as a teenager and thereafter continued to self-medicate his depression. There were early signs of trouble that I chose to ignore or minimize.

Bob didn't drink Black Velvet whiskey very often. It seemed he would do it when I was away selling some of our products. He could be wildly creative on those occasions. Two products he made this way come to mind: the detailed and elaborate newel post and the Mount St. Helens window installed in the honeymoon shack.

That volcano erupted in the eighties. Bob and I made a trip to Denver and Boulder, Colorado, to buy stained glass. There was a new product, a ripple glass made from recycled glass. It was more uniform and easier to score and break than some of the other, fancier glass. He used this gold and orange glass in the window. The way these pieces burst up through the design reminded me of the eruption in Washington state. I gave the window its name.

A Turn to Nature for Respite

There was a day in September when Bob was building the glass-bevelling equipment. He had gone to Consort to get a piece or some information from the machinist. I expected him home by lunch. These trips didn't usually last that long. It was a Saturday; my sons were helping the neighbours with their cattle.

I plodded the dirt path to our honeymoon cottage and went inside. I tried to push back the thoughts that were troubling me. I confided in my journal and then put it away. I decided to go for a walk.

The crisp prairie wool crunched and broke under my feet. I noted prairie flowers past their prime and now gone to seed. The dry, dusty days had greyed their leaves. I knew most of them by name. They had the drought-resistant silver leaves of sage, mallow and another plant I can't find in the dictionary.

I eased my way through the limp fence, careful to keep my dress from snagging on the barbs. Zeke, the big shepherd–coyote mix, slipped under the wire to ramble and explore. I checked the neighbours' pasture for signs of cattle ranging. I also looked up to the two big rocks on the south horizon.

I stopped to admire a solitary buckbrush plant. All its leaves were like tanned leather and had rust borders. I found two pieces of bleached willow post from a long-forgotten fence line.

My feet felt the crisp lichen and dry grass as I approached the brow of the hill. I reached the hill's crest and was accosted by a thousand buzzing insects. I heard the loud hum of grasshoppers and other insects crouched in the tawny grass. I scanned the valley and looked for the creek. I saw the lush green beside the water and made my way through the scarlet beauty of prickly rose bushes. Zeke leapt into the mucky water and returned to my side before shaking off the water.

On the way back, I picked a souvenir here and there to put in my wicker basket. As I neared the acreage, I paused to admire our handiwork. The dark cedar stain of the structures we'd erected or improved contrasted with the evergreen and autumn colours.

The next September, Bob was hospitalized for lung congestion. He stayed in bed until noon for days at a time. I couldn't budge him from his depression. Sometimes he would get out of bed and swing into action to get a load off the truck so he could go to town for a case of beer.

In the story *Vanished in Darkness,* Eva Brewster describes searching for her daughter. Eva had been taken into a concentration camp with her husband and their little girl. They were all separated immediately. The whole time she was there, she hoped to find her child. I was really absorbed in this story. I was saying, "Take me. I want to be your daughter."

Eva's story was unfolding during the Second World War, which was also the time when I was separated from my mother. I was an adult reading that true story and feeling myself finding my mother. She was in an institution, the mental hospital. My mother's experiences there might have borne some similarities to Eva's. I cried tears that I had stored for a lifetime. I experienced catharsis that summer of 1984 when I read *Vanished in Darkness*. Eva's was a story of survival.

And now, when I tell you this again, I know how deep that wound, that breaking of the bond between me and my mother was.

I read that book when I was deep in the middle of a very troubled relationship with Bob, who was suicidal. It has taken me all of these years to finally look into the pictures I have of Bob and of my mother, and to see that same look of sadness that each of them carried in the last year of their lives. I was in both pictures, standing beside them. I realize that I was drawn to Bob because I still hadn't healed from the loss of my mother.

Building and Construction

While Bob was having his bouts of depression and addiction, my sons and I coped with living on a construction site. This went on for seven years. Bob used the bricks from the old telephone building to line an addition to the Bullick house. It increased the size of our bedroom. The frame was constructed from old bridge timbers. It held a fireplace enclosure and a chimney. The floor was black slate of random sizes. I liked that addition so much that I insisted we keep it when we tore down the old house. It was incorporated into the new house. That chimney still stands on the property.

When it was time to raze the old house, Bob built an addition to the double garage we used as a shop. This became a bedroom for my four sons. There was a cedar-lined shower, a toilet and a sink. Bob built a brick enclosure for the wood heater I had gotten from the home place where my brother Harley farmed. The brick absorbed the heat from the fire and released it during the night. There was also a fan that took away some of the heat and distributed it to the rest of the shop.

Bob built a cedar-lined room with edge-wood fir flooring. More of the fir was used for counters. The stove, sink and table completed the room. There was an interior water-glass-panelled window above the table that allowed light to filter into the back of the shop. We made many multipaned window frame purchases from the lumberyard that has since closed in Edmonton.

Bob superinsulated one of the grain bins on the western edge of the acreage, and this became the honeymoon cottage. He installed the Mount St. Helens window in the south wall. He added a porch on the east side to serve as an airlock so outside cold didn't come in every time we entered or left. We slept there in the heated waterbed. We were warm enough with heavy wool quilts on top and no extra source of heat. We slept there winter and summer.

To further our stained glass business by developing new skills, Bob learned to make hand-bevelled glass in Denver, Colorado. He discovered what machinery he would need and built all of it himself once he returned. He consulted with a machinist or millwright at Consort.

Bob designed and built an energy-efficient Victorian-style house. Rob Bullick helped us calculate the roof lines. When Rob went home for the weekend, Bob had me up on the second floor with 16-foot lengths of two-by-fours. He calculated the roof lines for the cupola that would grace my upstairs office. When the room was completed with its raised dome, I said it was to accommodate my lofty thoughts.

There was a third storey in the peak of the house. That room was 12 feet by 20 feet. Bob laid the bricks for two more three-storey chimneys. The first chimney was the one made with telephone office bricks, which was included in the brick-lined addition. All of the bricks were secondhand, which are actually more expensive to buy than new.

He designed metal blades and cut them with the carbide blade of his saw. These blades were installed in the four-sided planer for a run of hardwood mouldings that would be produced for the coffered ceiling. The newel post and French doors were works of art. The construction was labour-intensive.

I would clear the breakfast table and wash the dishes and walk over to the new house to find out how I could help. I wanted his company. Many days he saw my intrusion as judgmental monitoring. When I thought he was working the program and staying sober, he would tell me he had spent a whole day drinking in the basement.

Bob also designed and built rounded and oval window frames. He had the tools to build stile-and-rail doors, so he produced our French doors using glass from older stained glass windows.

After the panelling was installed in our Victorian-style mansion, the wood was stained and then spray-lacquered. The mouldings were stained and lacquered and then worked into the intricate coffered frames for the white tin sheets we got from Stubbs' Grocery Store.

The water heating involved multiple zones, so a whole wall of the furnace room was adorned with copper pipe. Bob also pulled wire, which is what he called the electric wiring. Neighbours helped us lift the sheetrock ceiling panels for the greenhouse. We laid the ceramic tiles in the greenhouse's heat sink at the front of the house. Interior bricks also absorbed the heat of the day.

Bricklaying was a specialty. Bob had worked for a bricklayer sometime in his youth; he had mixed the mud and brought it to his boss. Soon that became my job. When we worked on our chimney, I was on the sloping roof above the greenhouse portion of the house. When he started piling metal milk crates to continue laying the top of the chimney, I told him he would have to find someone else to be a witness to calamity.

Bob was contracted to create a number of fireplaces and estate signs. Sometimes he would build an entire interior wall of brick for someone's rumpus room. He designed and built gate signs for many farms in the area. These signs included the brick portion plus a sandblasted cedar wood sign that displayed the family's name.

Tough Sledding

Bob and I celebrated New Year's at a 12-step recovery function in Stettler. It was a call-up meeting. I spoke about the tough sledding I had experienced in the past year of 1984. I was looking forward to some smooth sailing in the year ahead.

I didn't think I deserved happiness. I lived those seven years with the threat of suicide. Bob's addiction continued. My sons also suffered. After hockey practice he left them waiting in the truck outside the Royal Crown Hotel while he drank inside. I had stayed too long in the numbness of my abusive relationship and was now looking for answers. I had left for a few weeks in June of '85 after registering for the Women's International Peace Conference in Halifax: the Voice of Women was celebrating 25 years.

The Peace Conference

Attending the Peace Conference was another life-changing event for me. I was the first to see the two rainbow rings around the sun at noon on the third day of the conference. Three of us with ties to Alberta decided to skip the crowded line-up for lunch. We found fruit and snacks at a convenience store on the campus of Mount St. Vincent University for women, where the world conference was being held. We were sitting on a bench outside when I looked up and saw two rainbow circles around the sun.

Ronald Reagan was President, and we were convinced that he planned to escalate hostilities with his "Star Wars program" in space. Big Brother was watching us and our peace and freedom were threatened. My wish was that the double rainbow was a sign from God, telling us that there would be no more war. I asked a Native woman if there was a prophecy that would explain the phenomenon we saw in the sky. The rainbows lasted for two or three hours.

When the conference was over, I had to be gentle with myself. Some Nova Scotia women had made and donated quilts for the generals so that they might have a peaceful sleep. One woman from Belize had been detained at the airport. We were afraid that the US spy network was taking a dim view of our peaceful activities. I felt like I had to go undercover. I would be safe if I were under one of those quilts.

The Peace Conference was the first destination of my travel that June. The changes in weather in Nova Scotia were new to me. I stayed in Chester the first night out of Halifax.

The waterbed I tried to sleep on never did warm up. The mail truck arrived under my window at four in the morning. When I walked around the town in the middle of the day, I could hear owls hooting in the trees because the trees were so big and dark inside that the owls must have thought it was nighttime. I was fearful when the wind came from the ocean at five o'clock.

I wanted to talk to Bob's parents. I was trying to understand why his life was spinning out of control. I thought a visit with my friend at Advocate Harbour, also in Nova Scotia, would help me in my search for sanity.

The bus trip to Parrsboro was a long one. I felt a strange energy during my stopover at Truro while I waited for the next bus. That changed when I felt trusted and valued. In two occurrences: a man asked me to watch his young daughter while he used the washroom. This was new to me. I wasn't a grandmother. I was only 45 years old.

At Advocate Harbour, my friend Jim had established an old-timey farm that hearkened back to my grandfather's farm. He had a few sheep that would get spooked for no apparent reason. Jim was digging a potato patch in deep loam. I know he had milk and had made cottage cheese. I found an old farmstead with an old Buick like the one I first drove on the ranch. That was where I came across a patch of horseradish. I got a spade and dug some up to flavour the cottage cheese.

A couple from Castor was also spending time there while I was visiting. Jim's place was above the Bay of Fundy. The couple would go each day in rubber boots to dig clams when the tide was out. We had a party to which we had invited neighbours and for which we had made a big stew with rabbit and clams.

When I was ready to leave, the couple drove me to Amherst to meet the train. I don't have a map in my head to show my travels in New Brunswick, but I do know that I travelled by ferry across the Bay of Fundy twice. I think I wanted to see as much of the Maritimes as possible while I was there. I was fearful when I heard mention of the tidal bore. I visualized being caught in tornado of water. At Digby, at a bed and breakfast, I ate and enjoyed one entire lobster.

A dense fog at the Fredericton Airport had everyone delayed and unhappy. The only bright spot was a row of women in booths providing rental cars. I became interested in some sheets of plywood delivered to the airport, and I was distressed when I learned that these would be used to separate these women from each other. I phoned the Department of Transportation to object. It felt like my energy had lifted the fog so I could get on my plane to Cumberland Head in upstate New York to visit Bob's dad and his brother, John. His mother was in Springfield, Massachusetts. I went there, too. Maybe, in retrospect, my search for sanity was a little insane.

The last stop for me on this eastern excursion was the National Convention of the New Democrats in Ottawa.

A Slippery Slope

Bob met me at the airport in Edmonton. He had taken out a new loan to buy an ancient power sander, which he had loaded on the back of a three-ton truck that he had borrowed. It was a major undertaking just unloading it from the truck. We never did get it operational. To me it was a monstrous piece of cast iron.

When I got back home, I found out that Bob had arranged for his own voyage of discovery. He was going to the

Philippines. He was gone from home longer than I had been. I received a letter from him before he arrived home. In it, he told me that he had found a new wife.

I met him at the airport in Edmonton. For a while, I was upstairs watching an American Airlines plane unload. I think it was his plane. It arrived earlier than expected. He had been gulping down three whiskies while I thought he was tied up in Customs.

He showed me pictures of the woman he wanted to bring from the Philippines. This sort of thing may not sound so unusual today, but at that time it was highly unusual. She was Catholic and would not come to Canada unless he was divorced. We sent away to New York for our marriage certificate. When it arrived, I found it was dated September 13, 1985.

Also after Bob had gotten home, he found out that the town wanted to have him build the brick and sandblasted sign he had designed. He went to work laying and pouring the footings and foundation on the west end of the town. He was frustrated when it rained and he had to wait to do the bricklaying.

The 10 days following his return were very tense. At one point, Bob asked me to use my acupressure massage skills to help him relax. I took off my rings and left them on the south windowsill of the greenhouse. I set up the folding massage table I had made from plywood.

Somehow he had gotten a prescription for Ativan, a strong benzodiazepine.

I went with him when he drove to Veteran to buy a case of beer. As was his usual practice, he drove and opened a beer before leaving town at the north end. We took the back roads. We had the old flatbed truck he used for some of his bricklaying jobs. The rain had stopped him from the town sign project. Roads were slippery.

When we arrived home, we continued drinking in the greenhouse, the south-facing room where Bob had installed the hot tub. We were listening to records. He put on "Take Back the Night" by George Benson. I noticed that he was drinking three beers to my one. I knew we were walking into dangerous waters.

At one point, he was so angry that he raised a beer bottle and aimed it at the four-by-five-foot stained glass Poppy Fantasy window above the hot tub. I tried to stop him. Then I gave up. He was stronger and more determined than I. The bottle landed at the edge, not in the middle where he had aimed it.

He was instructing me in matters relating to his death. I managed to get the Castor doctor on the phone, who said he wanted to talk to Bob. Bob said something negative about the doctor, but I convinced him to take the phone anyway. I'm not sure what was said when they spoke. When the police arrived, Bob was sleeping upstairs. I didn't want to wake him. I was afraid he would be belligerent with the policeman.

The next day, he broke the coffeepot when trying to make his morning coffee. When he threw the pieces into the corner of the bathroom instead of picking them up, I could see that his former pride in his achievement—the construction of our home—was now gone. He didn't care anymore. It might have been an effect of the drug he was taking.

There was so much happening that it all became a jumble of insanity to me. It was nearly evening, and Bob was talking about killing himself. I knew we had guns on the property. He went to the place in the new house where the shotgun was stored. I was with him. He decided to leave it there. I was afraid to leave him alone.

I followed him to the honeymoon shack. Seemingly from out of nowhere, he had a gun in his hand. It was the high-powered rifle. I tried to wrestle him and pry it out of his hands. I had gotten my hand to the trigger when we were pointing the rifle to the ceiling. I wanted to find out if there was a bullet in the chamber, so I pulled the trigger. The gun discharged into the cedar. Bob was surprised and looked up, concerned about the damage to the ceiling. We still held the gun. He hit me hard on the cheek, and I fell to the bed. Now he was afraid he had hurt me. He left, and I tried to hide the gun.

I went to the shop, where I found Doug and Tyler. There, I hunted for the ammunition for our guns. I put the bullets in the deep-freeze.

The next day I put in an urgent call and made a Friday appointment with a mental health worker in Stettler. My doctor had already made a referral for me. I had been waiting for weeks. That day I wanted her to see Bob, however. I was at my wits' end. I was hoping to get him into Ponoka.

Bob and I drove to Stettler. The mental health worker took me into her office while Bob stayed in the waiting room. She told me that I had to look after myself. She didn't want to see him. While I was talking to her, he went across the street—to a dining lounge, I think it was—to get some alcoholic drinks. I found him there and drove us back to Coronation. He wanted money to buy more booze. When I wouldn't give it to him, he made a deal with the owner of the Tasty Mill to borrow money.

Bob was in grave danger and distress, talking about suicide. We saw our neighbour on the road as we were returning to the acreage. I stopped so Bob could talk to him. I hoped he would come to his senses, because I was running out of solutions.

When he got it into his head that he was going to die, it was like he was already a dead man. He said that he had made a suicide pact with the woman he had met in the Philippines. I was paralyzed with fear, and he couldn't think of anything else.

Adam and his son, Doug, had moved to our acreage at Bob's request. Adam had been a heavy drinker and was trying to help Bob get sober. He was dying of cancer. They were there at the acreage that summer while Bob was away at the Philippines. Adam was now in hospital in Calgary and seemed to be dying. He had to have fluid removed from his lungs.

My friend encouraged me to leave and go with him to a 12-step recovery roundup in Medicine Hat. I was fetching a laundry basket of recently bought clothes to put in my car. I thought I might have to stay away for a while. Bob was drinking rye whiskey and beer, which he had bought with the money he had gotten from the Tasty Mill. When I left, I forgot my purse and the basket of clothes. From Coronation, I phoned my friend in Calgary. I told him I had forgotten my purse. He said that I shouldn't go back for it. He would meet me at Brooks, at the Petro-Canada gas station and restaurant.

I drove and drove as it was getting dark. It was September 1985, and Highway 36 was under construction. The road seemed endless. I had to manoeuvre around the muddy puddles and broken, rough gravel. I waited at the restaurant for my friend. He drove me to Medicine Hat.

That night I saw police cars driving past our motel. They might have been looking for me. They called me on the phone the next morning and wanted to know if I was alone, because they had bad news. That is when I found out that Bob was dead and our house had been burned to the ground.

I phoned a Medicine Hat 12-step member who had attended our meetings in Coronation and asked him to come and talk to me. I needed his support to help me handle this news.

I couldn't leave the roundup right away. My car was in Brooks; I was numb. My friend read "How It Works" from the Big Book to open the noon meeting. An alcoholic told his story. It helped me to hear that he had been suicidal and had gotten the help he needed. He was alive. I was high in the bleachers of an arena listening to a woman's story. I felt both encouraged and better when I was paged.

I had to go home to Coronation and face the wreckage of my life. My sons were starting to doubt that I was alive. The grasshoppers were thick on Highway 41 as my friend drove me back. I left my car at Brooks. My sons brought it back later.

When Bob had phoned his mother, she was on call at a suicide helpline in Springfield, Massachusetts. He talked to her for 14 minutes while the propane was turned on and filling up the house that he and I had been building for seven years.

When he hung up, she phoned Allan Chinnery, whom she had met when she visited one summer. He got to our house in time to hear the explosion. Thinking that Bob was dead, Allan put Doug in his truck. Bob then crawled into the truck. They drove to Coronation Hospital. Bob was severely burned and died soon after he got to the hospital. Doug had tried to stop Bob when he was lighting the propane in the furnace room. He, too, was badly burned and was taken to the same hospital in Calgary where Adam was being treated.

He Came and Went

He came with two zip-together sleeping bags.
He said it was okay to leave food on my plate.
He taught me how to sit and do nothing,
Or to play cards or watch music videos or listen.
He showed me how it wasn't my fault
When he slept all day or was sad or drank.
He used his hands and mine to make
beautiful things.
It wasn't my fault when he left
And didn't leave the zip-together sleeping bags.

—Lavera Goodeye, 1989

Bob requested that he be cremated and his ashes scattered at Coronation. I'm not sure if we had worked out just where they should be scattered. Bob and I had visited Fred Tinio, the Philippine minister of the United Church. Bob had wanted to talk about his trip to the Philippines. The minister and I hadn't known that we would be planning Bob's funeral a few days later.

I went to Edmonton to meet Bob Sr. and Steve and Jamie, who flew in from Alaska. We all met up at Bob's aunt Mary's place. Bob's dad wanted to go on to New York to be with the rest of his family.

Mary's ex-husband was also living sober in Edmonton. I asked him to read "How It Works" from the Big Book of Alcoholics Anonymous. He and his wife brought Mary to the funeral. I brought Steve and Jamie home with me.

Bob's cousin came from Calgary with his wife, Tamie. My sister Joan brought Bob's ashes from Calgary.

I didn't ask anyone to sing at the funeral. I was so surprised and pleased when Shirley McLarty and Shirley Tinio sang a beautiful, touching song.

I didn't write an obituary for the paper, either. It was just too difficult to find the words. Someone else wrote it better than I could have written it. Bob is still valued for all the beautiful stained glass pieces we sold and displayed at fairs and parades. Many people had come and marvelled at the Victorian-style house he had designed and built from the ground up.

I didn't phone our friends Cory and Brian in Edmonton. I just couldn't tell them that Bob was dead. I'm sure they would have come to the funeral. I did eventually call them, and then I went to see them. I stayed overnight and had a dream. Bob was there in my dream. We were with some other people. Maybe it was a party. I tried to convince him that he didn't have to leave me, but he did leave.

Finding My Way at Hanna

The next August, I was living in Hanna and had asked some friends to go with me to the Nose Hills to scatter Bob's ashes. They didn't want to make the trip, so I went alone. Maybe I should have asked some of my sons. I climbed to the top of the Nose Hills. I wasn't sure which way to go, because I had never been there before. Upon reaching the summit, where the hill dropped off steeply to the south, I could see the Hutterite Colony we had visited many times.

I scattered my late husband's ashes in a spot from where I could see all the way to Coronation. I later planted a juniper up there in that place. I walked home another way when the sun was setting.

On September 13, 1985, Bob died as a result of the fire that burned down our house. I lost my husband and my business partner. Both the house in which I had invested and my husband had gone up in flames. I knew I had to heal. I was back at Coronation and found myself widowed a second time. I thought I hadn't gotten it right the first time. *I didn't learn,* I thought to myself.

Colin and Lee were finished high school and on their way to becoming responsible adults. When I couldn't find housing in Coronation, Kelly enrolled at J. C. Charyk High School in Hanna. Tyler was in Grade 9 and soon noticed all the little girls who were just waiting for him to pick one of them as his girlfriend. Our first home was in a west-facing suite at the Hanna Inn. I could see the Hand Hills from my west window. They were a substitute for the Nose Hills. The Hand Hills made a blue incline that dropped off to the north.

Hanna was a good fit for Kelly in his last year of high school. Kelly and Tyler adopted Hanna as their new home and later married Hanna girls and worked at the Sheerness power plant.

After the fire, and with the burns he received, Doug was in the Burn Unit at the Foothills Hospital. I think Adam was in hospice, so Doug was there, too. I visited them. Adam was much better than he had been on the night Bob died. He was available to encourage Doug as he healed from his burns.

Adam lived almost another year. By some strange coincidence, we met and visited at the Calgary bus depot in May. I had sold my Toyota Corolla to a Calgary woman and was catching a bus to go back to Hanna, where I had another car. Adam was getting on another bus to go to Medicine Hat.

We enjoyed a nice piece of time where we talked and caught up with each other. I sensed that he really needed to know how I was doing. I was so surprised to see that his cancer had allowed him to live this many months. He went home to die. He suffered intense pain as the cancer was ending his life. I went to his funeral.

Picking Up the Pieces

After Bob filled the house with propane and exploded himself into another dimension, I was left picking up the pieces. One of those pieces was the wood and brick sign for the town. The design was represented in an artist's colour rendition that already hung in the town office. The town didn't take long in finding a bricklayer from Big Valley to do the work. It was already past the middle of September. The bricks had to be laid before frost stopped the work. I asked a member of the Town

Council how they were doing the wooden part. He said that they would buy the letters.

The design showed the word *Coronation* in script, with the words *Welcome to* in block letters above it. This was to be sandblasted into cedar wood, and the letters painted white. I knew the artist's painting wasn't going to resemble the finished sign. I contracted with the town to produce an eight-by-five-foot sandblasted wooden sign.

I enlisted the help of good friends with whom Bob and I had worked while building our house. I had them stack, glue and bolt together the two-by-four boards and then haul the structure out to the acreage. They put it on two sawhorses in my shop and living quarters.

I painted the sign with three coats of white enamel. I used our offset projector and the town's picture so as to ensure the writing was large enough and closely resembled the painting. I drew on the rubber resist— also used by memorial companies to sandblast marble headstones—and used X-Acto knives to cut away the parts that needed sandblasting.

I also needed help loading the sign on the flat deck of the International when it was ready for blasting. For this task, I had made arrangements with M R Auto Body. We had known them, too, because of the times when Bob would get drunk and smash up the old Toyota truck. He treated it better after he had built a house on the back of it.

I set aside a day in spring when I could come and use M R Auto Body's sandblaster outside. I wore coveralls and a heavy breathing mask. I had to refill the sandblaster's canister with one bag of silica sand at a time. I was concerned that the weather wouldn't hold. There were clouds threatening me from above the whole time I was pointing the nozzle at the wood and watching it blow the slivers of cedar away. I had to work back and forth, making sure I didn't cut too deep. I needed time to finish an even job, but the storm seemed to be circling.

The first raindrops came while I was pulling a tarp over the sign. I eased it onto the back of the truck. I was really hungry, so I drove out to the Frontier Hotel for a burger.

Someone was saying, "That was a wild storm. Six inches of snow fell at Airdrie in just half an hour. They had to close down the airport at Calgary."

I asked, "What are you talking about?"

The person said, "We heard it on the radio. A blizzard just hit at Calgary."

I drove the sign out to the acreage and then drove the truck into the barn. I left it there until the weather cleared and warmed up. There was more painting and varnishing to do. I was living in Hanna at this time.

The storm continued for a few more days. One day I was driving out of town and saw the flags on top of Gene Kush's office hanging limp. I drove out to Spondin, where Kelly was working. I met a blizzard just a few miles out of town. Snow was drifting across the road. Hanna was in the eye of the storm, and the wind was intense out of town.

This spring storm caused widespread damage. The wet snow froze onto the power lines and pulled down miles of aluminum transmission towers along Highway 36. I saw this storm as a vessel for the anger I felt about having my whole life torn asunder. I created a storm that I hadn't planned.

The acreage where Bob and I lived was an oasis that enjoyed its own mini-climate created by all of the mature evergreen trees and the south-facing slope. In winter, butter left on the kitchen table melted in the winter sun. I would drive from a dry town and see that rain had come to our acreage while I was away. There was a generous pond in the poplar grove between the house and the shop. Ducks swam there, and frogs were plentiful. I woke when I felt something in my hair. We were sleeping in the basement of the new house. I lifted my head. A frog had plopped onto my pillow.

The summer after I had made the "Welcome to Coronation" sign, I attended the Creation Spirituality Workshop at the ski resort in Big Sky, Montana. Some of the women who had attended retreats at the acreage in 1984 and '85 told me that Starhawk would be there. I took the mobile mansion gypsy wagon Bob had made and was the only nonresident attendee. I slept in the wagon in the parking lot. I could look out my back door and onto this marvellous mountain. I was learning about ancient and modern witchcraft. When I thought the Christian God would punish me by striking me with lightning, I reminded myself that the earth grounds lightning.

I was also enrolled in a poetry class, where I wrote my poem "Woman Rising from the Ashes."

Woman Rising from the Ashes

Despair tore at my breast. Dreams lay
crumpled and crushed on the ground.
My skin was cut by agony. Tears gushed from
my deepest being. My body, trammelled
by death. Fire lashed the core of my
existence. Fear and uncertainty plummeted
my spirit.

Silent, alone, I struggled. Searching,
looking, straining, for a flicker of life.
Solitary, fragile, trembling, raising one
finger to touch hope.

I fell back, sinking low into the
smouldering ashes.
I saw a light, felt an embryo of warmness.
A tiny seed of power began to stir. An atom

of energy expanded and gently burst.

The mother mountain nursed and tended
this little fraction of wounded, hurting
creation.

The nymph that I was sensed the sun,
the warm soil, the breath of humanity waiting,
caring. I made a squirm, a
wiggle, toward a glow I felt.

Somewhere a small door opened. I softly
stretched   forward,   upward.   The   universe
waited . . .

The labour was intense. The rebirthing
of a woman fallen into the ashes of life
was slow and painful. Dark hours of
pain ensued.

The winter of my journey faded and thawed.

Power and strength and beauty rose in
sunlit splendour. Shining love burst forth.

Grace and divinity rested on my smiling face.
The glow of life was again a burning flame.

—Lavera Goodeye, 1986

I used the image of the phoenix rising from the ashes
in this poem, which I wrote in the first year after Bob
had died. It was so early in my grieving process, and

I was creating a blueprint for my healing. I learned to honour creation and associated my body with the earth. I had the sense that seeds came forth from the earth and that life came forth from my body. I heard about the Native ritual of the vision quest and found out that I could attend one in the Sierra Mountains in California. It would take place during the week of September 13, one year after Bob's death.

I told my counsellor, Edna Jolly, that it felt like my whole life had been thrown up into the air. All that was left were the pieces of my life. She told me that I didn't have to catch them before they had time to land.

I said to her that the Creator really loves me. Look at all the lessons he sent my way.

Judy Collins called the story of her life *Singing Lessons.* One of her songs is "Both Sides Now." The hard lessons she had learned helped her to write about her feelings and sing some amazing songs. I read her book because I thought it would help me understand my alcoholic husband, being that her alcoholic son took his own life. *Singing Lessons* helped me understand myself as much as it helped me understand Bob. I realized that I was often more of a mother to him than a wife.

Bob had grown up in a family of people who had mental health problems. Perhaps he, like I, was looking for a mother. He was 13 years younger than I. His mother and aunt were troubled because their mother died and their father had deserted the family. Bob's grandfather on the other side had deserted his family and started a new one.

My relationship with Bob was so dysfunctional that it wasn't until after he died that I added up all the losses he suffered while we were together. Bob had four brothers. His mother came from a family of four girls, and these girls, once grown, gave birth mostly to boy babies. I think there was one girl.

Two of his cousins died. One of them, who had lived in Edmonton, suffered from allergies. After coming home from the hospital after a bout with his allergies, he overdosed on alcohol and Valium. Another cousin in Vancouver was gay and was an alcoholic. He had been drunk on his birthday and was run over and killed by a city bus. These careless drug- and alcohol-fuelled deaths were prequels to Bob's suicide.

The grandfather on Bob's father's side produced another family, two girls and a boy, Ted. Although Bob was born in Montreal, many of his relatives came to Edmonton and Calgary. Ted was an environmental lawyer and practiced in Edmonton for a while. He visited us when he was leaving for Halifax, where he would marry another lawyer who taught at Dalhousie University. When I first saw Ted, I was frightened. I could hardly look at him, my reaction was so strong. It was like I had a premonition of doom. Ted drove all the way back to Nova Scotia, possibly not stopping to rest. He was at Amherst when he crashed into the back of a low-boy truck and died.

I attended a suicide prevention workshop at Coronation in the fall of 1985. Bob's suicide was still so fresh in my mind. I had many questions. I had also experienced the suicide death of my mother when I was young. There were two presenters at the workshop, a man and a woman. Each one of the people who attended had experienced the loss of someone close to them by way of suicide. We all had questions and wanted answers. We did acquire more knowledge at the workshop. It helped me to learn that I couldn't blame myself, but I could intervene when I thought someone was planning a suicide. The presenters told us about the warning signals of suicide, saying that these may get our attention, at which point we should ask questions. We shouldn't be afraid to ask someone if he or she is thinking about taking his or her own life. If the person has a plan, then there is time to intervene. Sometimes, people in emotional turmoil have tunnel vision and feel they are out of choices. They can't see ahead.

I found an opportunity to do some volunteer work to bring better mental health services to our area. I joined the Hanna and District Mental Health Association and did everything I could to establish Family and Community Support Services (FCSS) for the County of Paintearth. In 1984, when I was running in the federal election, I discovered this program at Killam and Flagstaff. I organized presentations and meetings to get the funding, and I also chaired a steering committee to get FCSS started.

As part of my preparation for establishing FCSS in my area, I went to an addictions conference in Calgary, where I met Judith Carle, who spoke about suicide and suicide grief. She introduced me to the book *Left Alive*. I read it while Bob was in the Philippines in 1985. It was about being left behind when someone you cared for committed suicide. This book inspired me to shed a great number of tears, resulting in piles of wet tissues. Bob was still alive, but I knew our relationship was going downhill fast.

On the way back from the vision quest in California, I stopped in Nevada at the serendipitously named town of Lovelock. My truck had been heating up on the hot desert road. Another traveller there needed water for his dog. I noticed a vehicle with a plate that read, "No job, no boss, no money, no worries." A white-haired man wearing a black bowler hat was walking by. I asked him if the car was his. It turned out that he was 93 years old, legally blind and walking to the post office with a white cane. His name was Wes.

From that time and until he died, Wes was my pen pal. He sometimes wrote two letters in one week. One time I was in Stettler and had the bright idea to walk across the street and buy Wes a card. It turned out that that day was his birthday. He kept a picture of me on his television and talked to it to get my attention. That was the day I bought the card.

There were a few weeks when I didn't get a letter. Wes had come down with Guillain–Barré disease, had gone to hospital and then went to live with his daughter. He was determined to get well and send me another letter, which he did. One time I typed a letter to him on my computer, which he didn't like at all. He said there was no feeling.

Wes had told me that he had a nephew in Happy, Texas, whom he decided to visit. He did get to Happy, Texas, but he died in Oklahoma on his way home. His nephew sent the information to me.

Another stop I made on my way home from the vision quest was to visit my sister in the British Columbian Okanagan.

Autumn Colours Rage at Me

It was September 25 when I reached Alberta. The weather was uncertain, and I was trying to get back to Castor for a steering committee meeting for the FCSS. I was stunned by the flaming colours of autumn, which contrasted with the dark green spruce and fir.

Autumn's colours blazed their rage at me. Everything I saw was aflame with the aspens' golden orange and ochre. The wind rattled the metal roof of my Land Cruiser. Rain splashed against my windows. When I drove through the Bow Pass, the snow that was flying was an indication of bad weather coming on.

I stopped to vent my anger. "Winter is coming on, but I'm not giving in without a fight. Boy, is there a fight brewing inside me. The flames of some virus grind at my belly as shiny yellow mush hammers at my anus. Yes, it is time to grind my teeth and haul off and get mad.

"The aqua blue water of the dam churns away in the wind. Mist and clouds and rain shroud the big hills. Gloom would like to take over as the day slides into night. There is fire in those leaves outside, and there is anger in my core. The red fire is bursting out.

"Here I am driving my foot into the floorboards trying to make a meeting at eight p.m. Well, they can damned well wait. They have their ideas about how it should be done. Let them take charge for a while. I'm not done fuming.

"The bastard went and left me with all his damned lumber and debts and machinery that no one else would want to go near. The nerve of him! And how dare he treat me this way? All the plans we made together to match his damned talents and abilities. All the damned self-teaching he enjoyed while I waited for my life to begin.

"Well, it's damned well time. The colours are ripe, and it's time that somebody, just once, take notice of me and all I've done. Damn it. I've been doing for Father and husbands and sons and community. It's time for me now.

"It's time to blow. Whatever. Wherever. Whenever I damned well feel like it. I can blow this burg if I damned well want to. I can blow money, too. Why pussyfoot around and look after his damned interests? Why should I stay out there all winter so nobody takes off with the stuff? They'll get it for next to nothing anyway.

"Damn it. It is time for me. It is time for me to get mad and haul off and look after myself. I've had it with being Missus Nice-Nice.

"It's my turn. I went to California on a shoestring. I did it. I can do other things that are good for me.

"Damn him, anyway. How the hell does he get off being so damned selfish?

"Well, it's not half bad back here in my nest, with the rain coming down and my legs buried in the covers. The steam and rain spoil my view of water, rock and nature's autumn fire. It will rage on a few more days until snow falls. I, too, will rage on for a while. I can express it with my foot on the gas feed, bumping along the highway in my gypsy wagon."

The fall colours added fuel to my ranting and raving until night fell. The next day could be another fiery day of running around expressing my feelings in busyness. I had to come back into my own body and care for myself. I was wearing myself down by doing for others. The responsibility I took on would leave me emotionally bankrupt at various times in my life. I was feeling resentment because no one was recognizing me for looking after others while neglecting myself.

Soon, I was going to Calgary once a week and taking Family Life Education at the University of Calgary's continuing education program. I would get emotional during those sessions. I had Valium, which I could dissolve under my tongue at coffee break. I was learning about relationships and communication.

I left Hanna after that first year and returned alone to the acreage. I didn't want to take Tyler down into the depths of the depression I was feeling, as I was grieving Bob's death. Kelly was finished high school. I arranged for Tyler to stay on the Quast farm with another boy,

Buster. Kelly went to work there, so he and Tyler had another year together.

I still had Bob's accumulation of lumber. There was a huge pile of stacked dimensional Sitka spruce, which was supposed to be the densest, strongest and clearest of all softwood. It was used for airplane construction. On a visit to Oregon, I had the privilege of touring the Spruce Goose designed and built by Howard Hughes. On a test flight, he actually had it airborne. I was disappointed when our guide named some other wood that was used in its construction.

We still had a large quantity of honey locust wood stored in one of our sheds, too. I felt really sad about all the work and products and wood that was lost in the fire. The house was gone, Bob was gone. I wanted something tangible to recover out of all of that loss. I contacted a cabinetmaker in Stettler and asked him to make a table and chairs from the honey locust wood.

Calgary

At Easter, Kelly and I announced that we would move to Calgary. We independently decided to move there to receive further education. He would take courses in power engineering technology, and I would prepare myself for the position of coordinator of FCSS for the County of Paintearth.

I was pleased to be accepted into group facilitation training, which helped me continue my personal exploration and which also taught me how to help others. I volunteered and then worked as assistant to the coordinator of Calgary Widowed Services. When I thought our group would realize the establishment of FCSS, the Government of Alberta instituted a period of austerity and stopped funding any new programs.

When I didn't get the position of coordinator of FCSS for the County of Paintearth, I went to Sharon, the coordinator of Calgary Widowed Services. She told me that she needed me to work on the Youth Bereavement Program. So I moved back to Calgary.

Three years after the fire, I was living in Calgary. I often came out to the acreage on the weekends. I was astonished to see that there was no water in the barnyard slough bordered by willows. The sun had baked the mud into sections. White snail shells were beached on two of the mud dishes.

I had been learning Native ways and decided to bring some magic to restore water to this corner of Alberta. I had sage and sweet grass and a bowl for a smudge. I went out to the slough on a blazing hot day and found four stones to indicate the four directions. I'd hosted two women's retreats on the property, and city women enjoyed the privacy my acreage provided. I decided I should do my ceremony in the nude. Time stood still as I offered the smoke to the four directions. I offered my body as a burnt offering. I didn't realize how sunburned I was getting.

I went to the stained glass shop and heard the radio announcing a fierce storm. There were hail warnings for my area. Now I was sure that God was going to punish me. If the wind destroyed my shop while I was in it, then I would be cut to pieces by all the shards of broken glass. If I got in the car for my drive to Calgary, other dangers might present themselves. I knew the willow trees would bend in the wind but not fall on me, so I lay under the trees while the wind passed over.

On the way back to Calgary, I bought some Solarcaine. I went into a Stettler service station washroom and tried to put some on my back, but I accidentally left my lovely white leather belt with silver chains on it in that washroom. The rain was coming down pretty good as I neared Calgary. That was the year the Calgary Stampede was almost rained out. It was raining the day I went to the home of one of my university friends and had her put the medication on my back.

A Story of Letting Go

Another time when I arrived at the acreage, a lone hawk shrieked at me from dead tree branches at the south fence. It was good to sleep again in the country quietness. In the morning, I got up while it was still dark and started my car. I wiped the dew from the windows and then drove alone as rosy tints slanted across the sky. A coyote stepped unafraid from the brome grass in the ditch.

When I turned onto the gravel south of Coronation, a single hawk sat on a signpost.

Then I saw her. A creamy brown cow, almost like a Jersey, switched her tail. Silent and alone, she stood as a solitary sentinel on the prairie. Beside her . . . stones? Rubble? Buckbrush? I slowed my car and backed up for another look. No, some white. A calf? Two calves? No. It's red.

I saw a rib high in the air. The cow was waiting for . . . what? Her calf was dead. Two more hawks, quiet on the fence, waited like vultures to take what was not theirs. When did they eat? The calf was half gone.

When will the cow let go and get on with eating grass? When will she go to the others and pretend she has not lost what had come in the spring from her womb? She has four feet planted under her. Only her tail moves.

How long will she continue her vigil, how long ignore her need to get on with her life? When will she let go of her dead calf?

I started up again and continued to the waste disposal site, where I threw off bags of garbage. A hawk hovered there. I turned south where the post office used to be. Another hawk was on the fence. One flew overhead.

At yet another corner, a seventh hawk was using the yield sign as a perch. Down a road with a little bridge, a road I never took, a deer stood partly hidden by the willows. She watched the hawk.

Along the fences for a stretch of eight miles, the meat eaters waited for the gophers to come out or for the cow to go and eat. When I reached the pavement, I stopped to take the towel that had been keeping my coffee hot. *I can drink it on the smooth road,* I thought. I put in another of Bruce Fisher's tapes on relationships. The city waited. I had two appointments to get my body back in shape, one with a physiotherapist and one with a podiatrist. *I am a tenderfoot from the country. The pavement is beating my feet to bits.*

I thought of the men in my life. I wanted them to help move me back to the acreage. I wanted at least one of them to hold me and appreciate me for who I was. (I was not sleeping with any of them.) I regarded myself as very needy and vulnerable.

Are the men waiting to see when I will let go? Are they waiting to take what isn't theirs, without giving the love and caresses and understanding I want so badly? Are they simply waiting for me to let go of my lost love? Bob was the man I had sometimes cared for like a child from my womb. To him I gave the mothering I needed for myself.

Each Time

Each time I feel I'm fine,

Each time I think joy is here to stay,

Each time I say how happy I am,

A tear comes to say that sadness, too, is here

To be a part of my life.

Lavera Goodeye, 1990

158

Reflections

As I write this section, I am trying to be a part of my community at Coronation. The psychologist Christine Baldwin talks of belonging and not belonging in society, citing the subtle messages we receive that suggest we are at the edge. I remember a time when I was young and we slept three to a bed. The covers were falling off me. After trying to sleep on the edge of the bed on a cold night, and because I couldn't wrest away enough covers to keep myself warm, I fetched my coat and put it over myself. Someone told on me, and my parents therefore moved me in the cold west room, alone.

I also recall hearing Hazel's message to me: "You are going to have to leave." I was on the outside watching Grampa bouncing two little girls in blue on his knees.

I have to keep balance in my life. I express my feelings, and I decide if I belong. I can choose what I wish to support and value in my life. I can celebrate all the choices I've made and respect myself.

Yesterday was Sunday, and I went to church for the second time in two weeks. I now receive the *United Church Observer* and emotionally respond to some of the articles in it. I am relieved to know that other Christians struggle with dilemmas. The publication's type is too small for me to read long before my eyes give out, though. I return to church to heal the hurt I suffered at the hands of allegedly religious people. I return to the church for a sense of community. I hope to find and experience the love of Jesus and his people. I try to get past the harsh judgment and the bullying I continue to inflict on myself. I go to church and hear the words that name my hurt and tell me that I am a child of God, but I resist them. I still have trouble feeling the true meaning of the words.

It all brings me to tears. I am alone. I am not a child of God. I come short of his glory. I am not enough. I resist confession. I resist prayer. I hear this judgment inside my own head and find myself coming up short of God's grace. I don't feel forgiveness or the love of God. I don't give in. I don't surrender to God's will.

"Jesus Loves Me," an old song I remember from my childhood, starts me crying again. I cry all the way through the service at Extended Care. I don't feel loved.

When I watch programs on TV, I am reminded that people from Christian churches hurt Native people by taking children away from loving parents. The parents were terribly hurt when their kids were taken away. The family was torn apart. The structure of the society was broken. Elijah Harper is one of my heroes because he was brave enough to leave his community and become a member of the white man's legislature in Manitoba.

Native Studies

I attended a resume-writing workshop and produced a very professional resume on quality paper. I attended career decision-making sessions. I was a mature adult searching for a new career. Teaching positions were not readily available, as they had been when I was younger.

After two years of searching and growing, I applied to the University of Calgary and entered the faculty of Environmental Design. I thought that the Social Planning course would help me with my political aspirations. This program offered a master's degree, and I would be credited for my degree in education as I pursued the master's. I had wanted to work in Africa. But I earned a failing grade in my Development course. After one year in the program, I was disappointed when I was asked to leave.

I found another way to pursue a career in social planning. I fit in better with the faculty of the Social Work, so I decided to work in that area, building on my previous experiences and preparing myself for meaningful work. In my Community Issues class, I was encouraged to write a paper: "The Quest for a Feeling of Belonging to a Community" was its title. I discovered that my personal experience had value in the field of social work.

Suicide drew me into Native communities. Native individuals were contacting me and drawing me in. At the Creation Spirituality Workshop at Big Sky, Montana, is where I had heard about the Native concept of the vision quest. There was to be a vision quest camp-out in the Sierra Mountains in California. I had decided to attend because that week in September 1986 marked the one-year anniversary of Bob's suicide.

I was attending an African studies class when I learned that some Natives had been arrested. I drove my gypsy wagon to the Peace River area. The Woodland Cree were in the news because they were protesting the development that was disrupting their community. They didn't have a reserve, so they held no claim to their hunting and trapping lands and therefore could not defend them.

I read Rosemary Brown's study about these people, which was called "Rupture of the Ties that Bind." Brown had spent some time with the Woodland Cree, discovering how the roads and the hunters and the work for the men created trouble in the lives of the women and children. It helped me understand how change and transition can disrupt the psyche of an entire society or culture.

The hunters had a system of distributing meat to younger members of the community. When they delivered the meat, they would check in to make sure that the young mothers were not being mistreated by their partners. But when the fruits of the hunt were no longer available, the society lost its structure and its safety nets.

The men had jobs and controlled the money. Soon, the roads that brought the jobs also brought the alcohol. Brown's study showed how alcohol consumption distorts a person's ability to deal effectively with stress or loss. I certainly knew that Bob's drinking had increased the danger he posed to himself. Before I met and married Bob, I attended my first Native ceremony in Edmonton when I was attending university there.

At a social justice conference I had gone to, the Native presenter didn't show up, so a Mennonite by the name of Menno Bolt told us of the culture. The first Native person I met in Calgary was Bernard Bearshirt. He talked to me at some length at the Laundromat, mentioning that

I might be able to get a teaching position at the Plains Indian Cultural Survival School. I attended a workshop on suicide and self-esteem held at that school. I saw that this topic created a lot of stress in the young people who were in attendance. The girls were holding on to the spots just above their navels—the power centre of their bodies.

At a two-day session sponsored by the Alberta Pastoral Care Association, a Native speaker outlined how holding a ceremony after someone's death assisted Natives with the grief process. This held meaning for me because I had been using the four steps of the grief process to help my clients at Calgary Widowed Services.

Mourners would recall elements of the ceremonies and move through the steps in their grief process.

1. Accept the reality of the death—viewing and spending time with the body at the wake.
2. Experience the feelings associated with the loss— singing and telling stories while attending the memorial service.
3. Release the person who has died—lowering the body into the grave and covering it with dirt.
4. Connect with community and social supports— sharing food and feasting with elders, relatives and friends.

Three years after Bob died, on the anniversary of his death, I returned to the Nose Hills where I had scattered his ashes. I planned to camp there for two or three nights.

Scattered

Colours of pink and mauve in the morning sky,

Grey tones cover the hills,

And I say,

The waters have scattered the ashes.

I climb a high hill and look down

On shadowed valleys.

I say, *The waters have scattered the ashes.*

Dry hill grass where I scattered the ashes.

The waters came down.

Only five snowy pieces remain.

Lavera Goodeye, 1988

I gathered my things and prepared to walk down from the hills. I heard the screech of a big cat from a safe distance away. When I got back to the acreage, five deer left their sleeping spot and jumped the north fence.

When I was living with my sons in the townhouse in Calgary, I slept in the waterbed with the cedar frame, which Bob built for the honeymoon cottage. Each morning I would get out of bed before the sadness had time to descend on me. I carried an imaginary box with me. It was the size of the box that held the stereo speakers I had bought when we were establishing our home in Edmonton 10 years earlier. I didn't have coffee tables or lamp tables for my living room. I covered the boxes that held my stereo equipment with MACtac and used them for tables. This box was just big enough for me to crawl inside and hide from the world.

After a while, that box was gone. I didn't need to carry it with me anymore.

Around that same time, I heard a policeman talk about family violence. He was a speaker at a Women's Institute (W.I.) conference. I talked to him at some length after his presentation. It took that long for me to realize that I had been in abusive relationship.

The threat of Bob's suicide and his violent acts had kept me on an emotional roller coaster. He had busted two stained glass projects. One was a lamp, my first stained glass project, and the other was a hanging he had made from the delicate, fine antique glass from Germany. He killed my son's dog, having shot him with my first late husband's .22 calibre gun. Then he busted the gun. He shot a hole in another glass project and the window behind it. He deliberately drove the Toyota truck into a grove of trees. He went joyriding in the Nose Hills until he rolled the truck.

This is the first time I've written about these occurrences. I thought that I had to live with the emotional abuse because Bob was threatening suicide. His violent behaviour could have easily escalated into his harming me or my sons. I was in a violent relationship. It was important that the police officer had spoken to the women at the W.I. conference, as some women need to be shown how to identify the signs of trouble in their homes.

I met Carol while attending my Environmental Design class. We both took a creative writing course in the evening at Mount Royal College. She introduced me to the Valley Creek Cultural Camp near Arlee, Montana. There, I learned beading and also scraped a deer hide to make a hand drum with the rawhide. There were many days when we sat around an outdoor picnic table working on our projects and listening to stories told by Agnes Vanderburg. She had founded the camp when she realized that Native ways were being lost. Her nephew would shoot a deer, and we would cut all the meat into strips and dry them over a wood fire. The men would tend the fire.

One of our first jobs was braiding the sweet grass. Agnes lived in a small RV trailer. She took some of us to it, which is when I saw her floor covered with the fragrant sweet grass. (It would dry too quickly outdoors.) It was purple at the roots. We broke off these roots so that they could be taken back and replanted. Then we each picked out three strands and braided them.

Agnes told us stories while we worked. She told us that her father gave her some horses when she married her first husband. When her husband was beating her, she sent her horses away. They went home to her father, which is how he knew that she needed him to come and get her.

Lynn Dusenberry Crow was also leading us. She helped us build the sweat lodge, and then she led our sweats. The fire heated the rocks we had taken into the lodge. Once all of us were inside, the flap was closed so no light could get in. Water would be sprinkled on the rocks to make steam, which created intense heat. Some of the women were young, so we tried not to make it too hot. Prayers and songs were part of the ceremony. We came out and returned four times. Each time we emerged from the sweltering lodge, we would jump into the icy cold creek that ran through the trees.

When Bob and I were on the acreage, we sent away a deer hide for tanning. Somehow, the deer hide was lost, so the tanner gave us an elk hide as a replacement. At the time, we didn't think we had been cheated. I took that elk hide to camp, where Agnes helped me make a skirt from it. There were gunshot holes in the leftover pieces. From those, I made a fringed vest.

I wanted to honour the double rainbows I saw at the Peace Conference in Halifax, so I designed and beaded a pouch with the sun in the centre and two rainbows around it. Carol helped me make a dancing shawl with rainbow colours in the fringe. I also used rainbow colours in the crow beads I used to decorate my skirt and vest.

When Agnes died, Carol and I went to her funeral. A year later, we went to the Arlee powwow where she was honoured.

Two More Homes

I found an eighth-floor apartment when Kelly and Tyler moved back to Hanna. My balcony faced south toward the Mount Royal Hill, which held some very nice, large, old, Victorian-style houses. I was glad I didn't have to worry that I might want to jump from that balcony. I never was serious about taking my own life. I knew that a jump from eight storeys would be a total disaster and might leave a person alive but crippled.

I laid a dam with PVC pipe left over from hot tub installations and also put down black plastic. I scattered brick chips that I had brought from the acreage and made myself a garden of potted plants. The plastic held water so my plants could suck up the moisture when I was away. I had a small table and two folding green-and-white-striped chairs. I also had a second bedroom with a west-facing window. This was especially nice because I could sit at my computer with the light coming in over my left shoulder.

I hung my stained glass lamp over my dining room table. It is in my bedroom now. I was coordinating the Youth Bereavement Program at the time. Work was only a few blocks from my apartment. I didn't have to brush off the snow or scrape away the frost in winter because I had a place to park beneath the building.

I had a dream when I was living in that apartment building. A creature in full body armour made of heavy black metal was agitated and kicking and scaling its way down the outside of the building across the street. It stomped across the road and down the back alley, where it went out of sight. My partner said that it wouldn't be long now, and we went to bed. The dream was so real that I was in shock the next morning when I found the pillow beside mine empty.

I thought that that creature represented my anger leaving me. The dream also seemed to be a promise that I wouldn't be alone for much longer. It also had an air about it that suggested it might be a visitation from one of my previous mates. My partner had come to me and stood at my side as I watched the activity outside.

My apartment was so comfortable that I now wonder how Carol had convinced me to share accommodations with her at 1313 Bowness Road. She was a Wiccan practitioner and was drawn to the orange stucco and black roof—and the significance of the double 13 in the street address. There was a large upper bedroom suitable for group workshops. A curtained alcove held my bed. I could facilitate a grief support group. I wouldn't be holding my position at work much longer.

Carol had a son, Shawn, who was about 10, as well as a younger daughter. Shawn was the one who saw that the maple tree was in distress. There was a branch suitable for hanging a swing on, but the bark was twisting and breaking open. Soon the whole limb came down and filled the entire backyard. Our landlord came by, cut up the tree and left the logs stacked against the fence.

The people I met when I travelled with Carol provided me with the encouragement I needed to apply for positions working with Aboriginals in the northern part of our province.

On my lunch hour at the Widowed Services, I would walk to the J. J. Bowlin Building and up to the 10th floor where the Alberta Government posted open teaching positions for Alberta Vocational College. I had driven to High Prairie for an interview but hadn't been hired.

My resume stated my career goals:

- To work with Aboriginal adults as an educator/ counsellor.
- To support and encourage personal growth and excellence.

It also included a lengthy mission statement and related my experiences with Native healing practices. It mentioned that when I worked with the New Democrats, I had thought that social policy could eradicate poverty, but my current view was that community education and individual opportunity would better allow people to break out of the cycle of poverty.

I had chosen environmental design as a field of study because I wanted to do development work in Africa. I had also registered in African studies courses. I wanted to do a study of Cameroon because it is English and French, like Canada. I was disappointed when my professor asked me to choose another country because there wasn't enough printed information available about Cameroon.

I had a vision that showed an exotic cow standing and facing to the left. In front of that cow was a white wolf. I interpreted the dream to mean that I should work with our Native people in Canada before I went further afield in my development work.

Most days, I would walk through a small park that had a stream and a waterfall. One day, I saw two Native men standing on the bridge by the waterfall. Thinking that they might be Cree, I changed my direction, walked over to them and asked if they knew anything about the Indians in northern Alberta. One of them said that they weren't very friendly. The men of that tribe didn't like him talking to the women, he said.

I told him, "I'm not surprised. A handsome man like you could be a threat."

He gave me his phone number so we could talk some more.

When I phoned him, I found it curious that women would answer the phone and say he wasn't in.

When I finally got him on the phone, I invited him to come to our place. We hadn't yet tried building a fire in the fireplace, but we brought in the maple wood from the tree that had broken and fallen in the backyard. We used paper and kindling to light a fire, which was soon crackling and flickering and warming us.

That was the night Roger lighted a fire within me.

In November, he and I went to Edmonton and took two of his daughters with us to the Canadian Finals Rodeo. I hadn't been there for some time. We went again two years later in 1993 to celebrate 20 years of finals. I bought a purple T-shirt as a souvenir; it now hangs on my wall.

I helped Roger, my new companion, produce a two-page story that his grandfather had passed down to him. His grandfather had been eight years old and present at—and therefore a witness to—a gunfight that had occurred between two of his uncles. His grandfather died before he could publish the true story. It was part of early Calgary history. The wrong uncle was accused of murder.

My Positions in the North

Roger found a job posting seeking adult education workers at the Grande Prairie Friendship Centre. We were already attending Integrated Neuro Systems in Edmonton. The coordinator for the literacy program in Grande Prairie hired us for her project. It would start in the New Year, 1992.

When we were bringing my two vehicles and some necessities to Grande Prairie, we stopped to visit relatives in Wetaskiwin. I thought we should be resting instead of partying all night. Roger's sister and brother-in-law lived in a three-storey apartment building. At five in the morning, I went out to the Toyota and brought in the drum I had made in Montana. We warmed it up, and then Roger's uncle John beat the drum and sang a North American Indian song. I was surprised that no one came banging on the door.

Soon after that, the old man died. We went to Hobbema for his funeral.

We drove north the next day in a blizzard. I was in my red hatchback car while Roger drove the Land Cruiser with the house on the back. I could see lights behind me, and they were catching up. Roger was farther back. When the big truck passed me, I found myself in a swirl of snow. I couldn't see. I landed in the ditch and my car was buried in snow. Roger couldn't pull me out. It was late at night. We had to encourage a reluctant tow truck operator to come and retrieve the car for us. I had to stop again before we made it to Grande Prairie. There was too much snow against my radiator.

We moved into an apartment where we could look west onto an open lot. Roger and I would interview each new adult student who came to join our program. He was the counsellor, and I was the instructor. We also worked with Elizabeth, the program director. One elderly student couldn't read. She knew her numbers well enough to play bingo, however. She was raising a grandson and really enjoyed learning to read words and make a grocery list. Her brother had attended school, but she was too shy to do the same.

There was a tribal elder who worked with our students, too. I was used to making individual programs based on my experience with the special-education students I had taught in Edmonton. Our students were happy to have the opportunity to learn new skills and connect with others in this setting. I enjoyed my work with the students at the Native Friendship Centre.

On-site was a gift shop displaying Native crafts and beading. People from all over the north would bring their items for sale. Someone brought in a beautiful pair of high-top moccasins with a rose design beaded into the buckskin uppers. White fur rimmed the top edges. I bought the moccasins for myself and wore them with my elk-skin skirt and vest to round dances, powwows and ceremonies.

A Native elder visited the Friendship Centre to lead a talking circle. He started with a smudge, borrowing my box of wooden matches to light it. I was used to sweet grass and sage for smudging, but he burned fungus. When I smelled that smoke, I was taken back to prehistoric times when people lived through the cold winters on musty earth. I could feel the bodies wrapped in hides, sitting around a smoking fire.

When Roger and I were living in Grande Prairie, we drove to a frozen lake for a cookout. There we built a fire in the snow, upon which we boiled tea and cooked a steak.

Working on a Native Reserve

When our six-month position in Grande Prairie was drawing to a close, Larry Soto spoke to us. He was on the Band Council for the Sturgeon Lake Reserve. He asked Roger and me to work in the adult upgrading project they were setting up at the chopstick factory. We would start in September.

We rented a house in Valleyview for the first year. When our landlord decided he needed the washer and dryer we had been using, I decided we needed to own a home. I was able to take a down payment out of my Registered Retirement Savings Plan (RRSP), but I would have to return portions of it each year. The house I found had a north-facing picture window. It looked across the street to the swimming pool and park.

Larry helped Roger replace the carpet, and I sewed curtains for the dining room, which also faced north. When I was preparing to serve Thanksgiving dinner to my adopted family and two foster daughters, I was lonesome for my sons and their partners. I framed their pictures. Three of them were married, and Tyler was engaged to Laura. I hung the photographs on my dining room wall and then continued cooking the turkey and its accompaniments.

It seemed strange that the picture window was facing the north. In June, the horizon maintained its pink hue all through the night. Greenhouses had north-facing windows, too. My neighbour had grown a bountiful garden, as well as cucumbers and peppers, in her greenhouse. Every year she had her husband bring in more topsoil. When I dug my spade into our garden at the south end of our property, the hole halfway filled with water.

I began implementing a landscaping solution to the problem of too much moisture. There was a sandbox that wasn't getting much use. We brought sheets of slate that Bob had bought in Colorado. Through the garden, I dug a pathway to the back fence, piling soil on both sides. I scattered the sand, broke up the slate and paved the way to a bench at the back fence.

I cut a circle out of the lawn surrounding a crabapple tree. Then I took the turf pieces to make a grassy slope to join the lawn and the slate pathway. The excess water drained into the back lane, and I was now able to grow flowers on the raised soil.

There was still enough room to park my gypsy wagon. Bob had built wooden bumpers for the Land Cruiser. The words *Mobile Mansion* were sandblasted into the back bumper. I had a nest in that mobile home where I could prop myself on pillows and read on a summer day. We sold the Toyota truck and set the little house on ties, keeping it in the same spot beside the crabapple tree.

When Roger and I were planning our wedding, I was sewing ribbon shirts for him and his two brothers, who would be his attendants. I made my ribbon dress. My sister Joan carried my shawl. Roger's cousin from Hobbema was my other attendant, and she had her own ceremonial shawl.

We were married on June 18, 1994, in a ceremony that was officiated by a Native elder and that took place inside a teepee on the land of Evelyn Soto. My two Christian minister uncles were in the half teepee with us. My cousin took videos.

We asked a talented little boy to sing a song at the wedding reception and dance. My grandsons Clay and Luke were thrilled to see someone their age belt out a song. I asked my sons to serve the drinks. They were disappointed when they witnessed people's behaviour that night. They thought they should rescue me from the life I had chosen.

I believed that the work I was doing in the Native community was important. I was a family support worker and knew the families I was working with. Roger and I were also foster parents. Three teenage girls were part of my new family. If I wanted to have some special time with them, we would go to High Valley Restaurant for chips and gravy. I was also doing grief support work in the community.

Roger was a descendent of a band of Indians that had been led by Chief Papaschace. We met other of his descendents as we travelled in the north. Some lived on the Sturgeon Lake Reserve. We had a friend, Randy Lawrence, in Edmonton who researched Native burial sites. He knew that Papaschace had taken his wives and what was left of his band to Elinor Lake near Lac La Biche. Randy went there with us. Roger's family had also lived there beside Elinor Lake. Eventually we found the spot. There was a little depression where the house had once stood. Thistles now grew in it.

Our guide and host was a fiddle player. He had a fairly good idea about where to find Papaschace's burial place. While the men were talking and looking, I found some rose bushes, which were wild, and a big piece of rotting four-by-four wood. It was the cross that had marked the grave site.

We went to the home of an elderly member of Papaschace's band. Roger interviewed him in the Cree language, and I recorded the discussion with our camcorder.

We also held meetings in Edmonton for the descendents, hoping to establish a reserve or a band. They wanted to be recognized as legitimate.

Collision Course

I was doing family support work and sometimes drove young children who were in foster care to visit with their mothers. My duties also included driving mothers for supervised visits or taking a child to an appointment. On one such occasion, I had a young boy with me in the car in Grande Prairie when the snow was piled in the middle of the street to a height above the cars and trucks. A truck came away from a stop sign, and its driver didn't look when he got to the edge of the pile and pulled in front of me. I caught the back of his truck with my car. My air bag inflated to protect me from banging into the steering wheel.

That was my third collision. One happened while I was living in Calgary in 1989. I drove to Edmonton for a workshop with a Wiccan practitioner. The workshop was cancelled, though. I decided not to have an individual consultation with her. I was driving my friend Cory from West Edmonton Mall and passing through an area I had often driven through when we had lived in Edmonton. Cory saw that a woman was going to pass in front of us, but I didn't have time to react.

In 1992, Roger was in Calgary while I was visiting family and friends at Coronation and Fleet. I cleaned my car while it was heating up, and I had to clean it again before I left for Calgary. I should have known of the blizzard and stayed put. I wanted to know what Roger was doing. I couldn't get him on the phone. So I decided to leave.

Once on the road, I could see a vehicle behind me. The snow was blowing across the road and coming down hard, but I could still see that set of lights behind me. I knew I would have to make a left turn when I reached Highway 36. I was past Fleet when I slowed down so that the other vehicle could catch up to and then pass me. And, indeed, the truck did pull out and pass me. Then immediately there was a bang, an impact. I was hit from behind and landed in the ditch. Another car took the shoulder. There were several vehicles behind me. The woman who hit me was from Calgary.

Two more vehicles, driven by people I knew, arrived before the ambulance came. I also knew the people in the ambulance. They took me to Coronation Hospital. All I had was a cut on my nose. They had called my sons while I was in the emergency room, and my sons were really worried. I'd been in a car accident, but they didn't know how I was. I did know that I had suffered some damage because my arm went prickly.

I haven't had any serious accidents since then. I realized that I had to learn to look ahead on the highway of life as well as on the road while in my car. I learned to see signs of trouble ahead and also perceive that there were consequences for my actions and those of the people near me. The enduring muscle/neck/spine trauma from three whiplash accidents didn't appear until a few years later.

Life on the Reserve

One time when we went to the Flintstones' restaurant, I heard people referring to someone as Gloria. When I heard the woman talk, I recognized her voice. She was one of the Slemp girls who grew up at Fleet. I was glad to see her again and to know that she lived near Valleyview.

When my students were talking about their weekend plans, I heard one of them ask, "Are you going to the zoo?"

I asked, "Really? Do you have a zoo in the north?"

They were referring to the bar in the Valleyview Hotel on the main street in their town. There was a bar in the Valley Hotel on the highway, but they preferred this one in the centre of town.

Roger and I went to the sweats led by Evelyn Soto. He and I, along with Charlie, gathered stones and the poplar logs for the fire. We also went moose hunting, and I learned to help with scraping and tanning the moose hides. We helped clean the fish caught in the lake.

In addition, we attended community events such as wakes and round dances. We had a good connection with the Grande Prairie Friendship Centre. On one occasion, we took an elder—the brother of the woman I had taught to read—to a round dance at Grand Cache. We faced some dreadful roads on the ride home. The road went through a forest reserve; there was very little traffic on it. We were in a blizzard, but Roger got us safely home. Another time, we used that road when it was covered in glare ice with a layer of water on top. It was very slippery.

I attended a number of wakes and funerals when members of Roger's family died. Sometimes a fire would be tended day and night outside the centre, where relatives, friends and neighbours spent time with the body of their loved one. The funeral would be held in a local church, and all would go to the graveside. Sometimes the casket would be carried to the grave. Family members might shovel dirt onto the lowered casket. A community feast helped connect the family to the people who would support them as they grieved.

When I was a little girl in grade school, the Natives from a harvest crew would camp in the picnic area across the road from the Fleet store. A little Indian boy my size and age came to our schoolyard at recess. It could have been the same Indian I met in Calgary and married. This was my third marriage. I went into my relationship with Roger with high hopes for the future.

My Third Marriage

During my third marriage, I was working each day close to my partner. This time he was matching my skills. It wasn't the same as farming or the stained glass business. I had never had a husband who left each day to go to a nine-to-five job. Some might say that Roger and I were enmeshed.

Roger could hold a job and stay away from drinking for a month at a time. He was a binge drinker. Once his body had been without alcohol for a month, he felt the craving for it again. At one time, he said he was going to teach Natives to drink sensibly.

When Roger stayed out all night drinking or gambling, I would start packing all my necessities into my car, frenetically expending my angry energy as I carried my things outside. I was going to leave him, but I never could follow through. The house was my investment.

Sometimes I would go looking for his truck. It might be at parked near a house party on the reserve. When I knocked on the door, his hostess told me that I couldn't enter. Another time I went to the town he had phoned me from at 11:00 p.m. I found his young driver doing a back-and-forth circuit while waiting for Roger to leave the bar.

When Roger went to Grande Prairie with his uncle Jim, they didn't return home until after midnight. The casino would have been closed. I couldn't stand waiting. I went to the edge of Valleyview and waited in the snow beside the road for him to come home.

During summer, while on another trip to Grande Prairie, Roger disappeared with our friend Larry. I stopped in Debolt looking for them, but they weren't there. The night was almost over. I drove north to the Kleskun Hills, letting the time slide away from me as my feet crunched over the dry grass. I watched for animals as I hiked the hills. Then I saw the glorious sun slip into view, at which point I went back home, only to find Roger and Larry still missing. In the afternoon I went out to the reserve, but no one there had seen them. They eventually came home.

I was so frustrated by Roger's behaviour that I was looking for a program for myself. I found a 12-step program again, and the people there helped me. I was seeking something more involved, though—maybe a 28-day program. If Roger wouldn't get help, then I would. He was working for the Métis, and we had found an education program through Métis Child and Family Services, in conjunction with Alberta Vocational College. I went to Edmonton to take a course called Family Intervention and Youth Support. While there, I stayed with my friend Joyce Kruger.

The classes were very useful. I met Aboriginals from Métis communities all over Alberta. We received instruction for how to study. I researched and made a presentation about gambling on video lottery machines. I had an advantage over the other students, as I had written papers for university. I earned a grade of 100 percent on both of my papers. For the one, I had extensively researched gambling addiction. Written from the point of view of the gambler's spouse, my paper showed how family members and the community suffer from neglect and face a danger when involved with people who are addicted to gambling.

The other paper described the Native way of counselling. Its purpose was to show that there is a way to help the client find his or her inner resources.

The classes lasted four months. While I was away in Edmonton, Roger's drinking continued. One weekend I came home to Valleyview to find a variety of liquor bottles arranged on the deep-freeze, which served as a full-scale home bar.

When I completed the program, I did a practicum in Valleyview with the Native Counselling Services of Alberta. The director in Grande Prairie was supportive of my efforts. Eventually, this training would lead me back to Calgary, where I would facilitate parenting education for Natives.

When we were living in the north, we bought an old canoe, repaired it and painted it. I looked forward to paddling this canoe because I had fond memories of a canoe trip Bob and I had taken to Bowron Lake Provincial Park in B.C. Mel Sell, one of the hired men on our ranch, made a project of building a canvas-covered canoe and painting it red. The paint made it waterproof. We took him to the Burma Bridge so he could paddle along the Battle River to our farm. When he didn't arrive, we discovered that a rock had punctured his canoe, squashing his dream.

Roger and I bought paddles for our canoe and enjoyed paddling on some of the northern lakes. When we went to Swan Lake, we saw two families of loons. There were many moose tracks when we went there in the fall. We lost a fishing rod in a lake near Atikameg. I caught a trout in Honeymoon Lake.

I was familiar with paddling and manoeuvring a canoe from my time with Bob, as we travelled many days and did a number of portages on our Bowron Lake adventure. If Roger was in the back of the canoe, he liked to steer by planting his paddle. This sabotaged any effort I made to control the canoe. I started to think about paddling my own canoe.

On one occasion, we were fishing in a large boat on Sturgeon Lake. There were five or six other people with Roger and me. One of them was an experienced hunter from another community. He later went moose hunting with us after telling us that he never came home without a moose. We saw nine moose that day before we found the right one, a young one. The day we went fishing, Roger and I were frustrated with each other. Our rods weren't working right and we weren't catching any fish. I don't know if anyone else was catching anything, either.

First, I threw my rod in the water. Our hunter pulled it out before it sank. Later, Roger threw his rod in the water, and again the hunter grabbed it before that one sank. That is why we were so surprised by how fast our rod sank in the lake near Atikameg.

My Brother Calls Me Home

I started carrying a cell phone. A call came in from my brother when Roger and I were shopping in Grande Prairie. My father had died with Eunice at his side. My father was feeling negative 17 years earlier. He had lost interest in life until he started checking in on Eunice (his friend's widow). He went to live with her. When she came into his room at the hospital, it was like the sun came out from behind a cloud. His face would light up even though he couldn't talk.

He died Friday the 13th of September in 1996. Roger and I drove to Castor for the funeral. My sister Joan had helped with the plans. The family had asked the United

Church minister to take the service. My father had been a faithful community member and had attended many funerals. He was well-known and had many friends.

My dad's brother wanted to speak at the funeral. We knew that my uncle would be critical of my dad's failure to embrace religion the way he had. My uncle was well-known for expressing his prejudices when he spoke at funerals, so we gave him a minor role to play in the service.

My dad never divorced Hazel. On the day of his funeral, she felt a hand on her shoulder as a voice told her, "This is Johnnie's day." She let go of any resentment she harboured.

A curious coincidence involves the deaths of my two parents and my two husbands. My mother and my first husband died in different years on April 17. My second husband and my father both died on a Friday the 13th of September, but in different years. My mother and my husband Bob both died by suicide at the age of 32 years. In any event, I was very pleased that after so many years my father was interred beside my mother in the Castor graveyard.

A New Position in Calgary

I wanted the position with Native Counselling Services of Alberta when it became vacant at Valleyview. A fellow from Red Deer was hired, however. I was feeling overwhelmed. I went to a sweat held by Michael David and his partner, Shirley. There, I asked for help with my family. It seemed that the Creator knew my need better than I did. We were out and about somewhere when I got the call to come to Calgary for an interview.

I bought a new outfit in the SAAN store. It consisted of peach-coloured, cotton-knit, long-sleeved shirt with a scooped neck, plus a flowered rayon skirt to match it. It was my uniform for the interview and the job. I was hired as a parent educator in Calgary. While I was happy enough living in a small town, Roger and his family had never lost their love of Calgary. We put our Valleyview house up for sale and moved back to Calgary.

My new position involved working with Native parents at the Rocky Mountain Plaza near City Hall in downtown Calgary. A curriculum of 15 lessons made optimal use of my group facilitation and education training. My experience in the north helped me relate to the issues my parent-students were facing.

All the lessons began with an elder's prayer and by smudging each person in the circle. The elder also read the Native legend that teaches the qualities the Creator wants children to learn. It was important that each person in the group be valued. We finished each class with a potluck meal and a graduation ceremony where we handed out certificates of completion.

Roger and I rented part of a quadruplex while we waited for our house to sell. We did find a reasonably priced house in Dover, although it needed some work. The kitchen floor tiles were broken and needed replacing.

Roger had a young fellow helping him cut the linoleum so that it wouldn't be my fault when the measurements were wrong. We removed layers of paint from the kitchen cabinet doors and repainted them. There was a suite with a kitchen in the basement, along with plenty of room for grandchildren.

At Christmas, I was waiting for my husband to come home with his paycheque so we could buy gifts. I later learned that he had gambled it all away and was ashamed to come home.

As addiction to alcohol or gambling progresses, the addict will risk losing relationships, meaningful work and monetary security to get the substance or to perform the behaviour. The unacceptable behaviour increases, and disaster awaits.

At times, I looked to the Mother Mountain, which represented strength. I had left the powwow at Arlee, Montana, because a big storm had moved in and soaked everyone. The teepees that had been erected by experienced Natives withstood the wind and hail. One fellow used a ladder to erect his teepee, but it was blown down. I knew I wouldn't be able to dry my things in the Laundromats because there were so many people using them. I stopped at a vender's who was selling the seashells used for smudging. I bought one. I used a pottery dish for many years and still keep it for that purpose. When I taught the parenting class, we had an elder bring her shell for the smudging we used to open each day.

I knew that Roger was coming home from work in the north. The Calgary Stampede was happening, and he hadn't stayed at work long enough to have a stake for his gambling. He even wanted money to get home. For him, the stampede was the casino.

Near Fernie, I saw a mountain and a campsite. I stopped. The mountain was the study kind I call the Mother Mountain. It rose in a perfect triangle. It was like the one I slept under at Big Sky, Montana, in the summer after Bob died. I was tidying my van. It was such a mess. I had left so quickly after the storm.

I got back to Calgary and discovered that Roger had stepped over the line of what I would endure. I ended the relationship. I was two months into our separation when I started a new journal with a wolf on the cover. Each day I would write out my prayers to the Creator and the God of my childhood. It was my way of letting go and letting God. I was trying to write myself into sanity.

I wrote this:

> Lord God of my childhood, I am humble as I come before you.
>
> You were there all the time when I thought you had forsaken me.
>
> You were there as a gentle teacher when I thought I was being punished.

Hear my prayer of gratitude for all you have
placed in my hands.

I thank you for your gentle guidance.

Great Spirit, I trust you to put the words in
my mouth.

Thank you for all I have in my life right now.

Help me to stop being a rebel.

Help me to honour myself that I may act out
of my own personality instead of giving myself
away and getting lost in my relationships.

I was attending 12-step support groups and continued my
work leading the parenting classes while simultaneously
preparing for my divorce. I took my petition to the
courthouse during one of my noon breaks. The last thing
I did in the old millennium was go to the courthouse to
receive my proof of divorce. Once I arrived, I learned that
a judge had already granted it.

When my son Kelly phoned in October 1999 to tell me that
his daughter Cassidy had been born, I was asleep. I had
been working on my own labour of love—scrapbooking
late into the night—while Sandy was giving birth. I was
awake when Cassidy was born, and I was asleep at 8:00
a.m. when my son phoned to tell me of it.

In July 2000 I went on stress leave. I was 60 years old
and running out of steam. I wondered when I would

retire. I felt that my work would chew me up and spit me out. I was finding it hard to continue working with parents who were dealing with loss and stress.

Also, the organization that employed me was going through changes. Chester Cunningham had established the organization to help Native people deal with a court system that seemed to have stacked the deck against them. He had also trained other Natives to advocate for his clients from offices all over the province of Alberta. He had been the director for 35 years and then had retired. I didn't feel the support I needed from my administration. The insurance company refused to recognize my need for leave. Employment Insurance stepped in when my company's plan wouldn't.

I found a good counsellor at Native Addictions and attended a 28-day treatment program for substance-affected people that was based at Calder Centre in Saskatoon, Saskatchewan. I was afraid I would continue getting into relationships with people who were addicted to substances or gambling. My counsellors there helped me to break out of my shell of self-doubt and low self-esteem. I did learn to value my compassion. I also had to look at the judgmental expression of religion that had blighted my life.

I was starting to enjoy better physical and mental health. In 2001, I got into a walking program called Joints in Motion with the Arthritis Association. On Sunday, May 27, 2001, I walked 10 kilometres in two hours at the Annual Brooks Women's Run and Walk at North Glenmore Park in Calgary.

I had more time and energy for my grandchildren and so attended Clay's Pee Wee Hockey Provincial Championship games at Drumheller and his Boys' Steer Riding events at Strathmore Heritage Days. Clay scored 79 out of 100 on his steer.

Returning Home

I was living in Calgary after I had left my position as parent educator. Lee found a song for me. It was Rascal Flatts's "I'm Moving On." When I finally heard it on the radio, I was driving from my son Kelly's home in Strathmore. I had escaped my own place during an abusive episode with my current roommate, with whom I was in a relationship. I had to pull over and listen. I was in tears because this song spoke about my plight. It came to me at a time when I needed to leave Calgary. Lee was the one who came with his horse trailer after I sold my house in Calgary in the fall of 2002.

The song spoke of the entire journey I had taken throughout my adult life. It seemed that I was always moving on. I had "left the people and their faces" and moved to the city or to the north. I worked and studied in Edmonton and Calgary. I had immersed myself in the Native communities of Grande Prairie and in Valleyview.

The song told me that I was going home. I "sold what I could and packed the rest," and I also "stopped to fill up on my way out of town." I was the prodigal going home to the people who I thought wouldn't let me change. Most of all, I thought, *"Maybe I will find forgiveness somewhere down this road."* The song reminded me of my need to forgive myself for the choices I'd made.

I moved into a bi-level townhouse with a hexagonal window when I first returned to Coronation in 2002. I choose my dwelling place with care. I have my own approach to feng shui, feeling the warmth of a place with my body. Home is where the heart is, and home is also where my heart was broken more than once. Home is where my dreams crashed.

This community to which I have returned holds me and the people and events I have loved. Becoming comfortable again with the people I thought I had left behind more than 12 years ago is another part of making the transition.

Revealing who I am is the hardest. But I do this here and now, with this book, because I have for so long lived in the books of others. I have held on to books and read them slowly because I never wanted to let my relationship with the authors end. I'd like to achieve that same level of connection with my readers. I want to honour myself and the lessons I have learned, ultimately to emerge from my self-imposed retreat. I have a deep longing to be known for who I am. I have to be my own person.

At the Evangelical Free Church, I bragged about my ability to create storms and make rain. A fearsome wind came up that night. The maple tree in my neighbour's yard shook and trembled and swooped. Lightning flashed and thunder broke above my head. I thought that God was threatening to punish me for my audacity.

The next morning, I went out to survey the damage. Two baskets of flowers I had hung on my back deck were gone. I searched the neighbourhood but didn't find them. I walked out the north-facing front door and strolled down my walkway. I laughed. God has a sense of humour. There was a neat little pile of small stones, twigs and debris in the middle of one of my pavers.

The United Church is uncomfortable for me to attend because I had been a part of two funeral services there, both of which are etched in my mind. The greatest loss I experienced was that of my Christian faith. When I came back to Coronation, the church was celebrating 25 years in its new building. I was lucky to welcome other homecoming people at the celebration.

The minister who had said words of comfort when my second husband died came to the event. The two women, both named Shirley, the ones who had surprised me with a touching duet at Bob's funeral, were present at the anniversary celebration, as well.

The two people who had known Bob best created a new stained glass window for the church. I may think that I am alone, and yet others value Bob's life just as I do. Rob and Laurie Bullick designed and produced the window with images of a sunrise, a rainbow, a dove, stems of wheat and Alberta wild roses. Rob had been the one to help us with the roof lines of our house. Laurie had worked for us and learned stained glassmaking from

Bob. They, who were our good friends, had once gone with us to Fairview, which is in the north, to attend a conference about energy-efficient housing.

Help for Body and Soul

I go to the Bible to read the story of the Prodigal Son. Now I see it is a story of compassion. Maybe I, too, am worthy. My tears come when I see that I am a child of God. When Bob was dying, my friend shared with me the saying, "Let go and let God." Later, I took a different saying—"And then the day came when the pain it took to hang on was far greater than the pain it took to let go"—and, along with a flower I had coloured, put in my scrapbook. It seems to me that the Bible asks and expects too much. It has hurt me enough. I have done enough. Yet I don't feel worthy.

In the summer before my 70th birthday, Shelly, the mother of my rodeo grandsons, told me that one of her barrel-racing buddies had gone for alternative therapy and was back riding her horse and competing. She had avoided hip surgery. I thought it might work for me, too, so I asked for the name of the naturopath. In September, I received my first injections in Calgary. I found out that I could drive to Rimby on Saturdays so I didn't have to travel all the way to Calgary every six weeks.

I come to the computer not because I am in pain, but because I am awake. My morning pill has done its job. It is later in November. My alternative therapies are helping me get a good night's sleep. The injections I've been getting are already helping me. I was in such a good mood at the annual Christmas craft fair at Coronation, where I had been talking about improvements to my hip function. I cancelled my surgery date for March 24 to see if I could maintain the better functioning without having to have an operation.

In December, I had a setback with pain and couldn't sleep, so I cleaned my desk in the middle of the night. I don't know if it is the extra-cold weather with no wind or the tomatoes I've been eating in a bean dish. I had a consultation with a naturopath who told me that some of the food I was eating was causing inflammation in my joints.

I didn't do full-time work outside my home and business when I was married the first two times, but I did teach as a substitute. I learned how to use computers in Coronation when the computer teacher had many health problems. I was learning to work on computers with students in Grades 7 to 10. At that time, students had to type out lengthy code in order to program the computer to accomplish one simple task. My students would tell me that the programs didn't work. Often, they had added a period, forgotten a period or made some other little mistake that had gotten in the way. I found out that I was pretty good at detecting these errors.

I've been typing on various computers since that time. I've written university and college papers on many subjects. I've taken creative-writing courses. I've also kept journals in many places and for different purposes. I prefer not to spend much time with my old journals, which prop up my bedside clock. Many, many times I went to my journals when I was in distress, but now I can recall enough of my pain without consulting my diaries.

I have learned to be assertive in relationships and also be mindful of what my needs are. I've used my life to be helpful to kids who feel helpless and can't read. I've been an adult educator and a grief support worker. I returned to Coronation after many adventures and now choose to call it my stomping grounds. This book describes the foundation I laid in childhood and from which I approached my adult life, and it also makes some connections between who I was in the past and who I am today. As I write, I struggle with diminished mobility because of calcium deposits in, and wear and tear on, my hips. While I heal from the pain of the conflicts I experienced earlier in life, I am hopeful that medical tactics will heal my body.

The Shantz name played such a role in my young life that I was pleased to see that our minister at Trinity United Church in Coronation was Steven Shantz. I asked him if he was related to the Ray Shantz, who was the minister at Markham. He said he wasn't. He also said that his father had chosen the United Church, so I thought there might have been some Mennonite in his heritage. I talked to him because he was moving back to Ontario and I needed to process the feelings that flooded me when I attended church. I told him of the two deaths and the two funeral services held in that church. The second service took place in this new building.

My plans for writing last night disturbed my ability to sleep. I have to be as courageous as a bullfighter. Oprah Winfrey had once asked Whitney Houston if she had any regrets about what she had revealed in her interview. Whitney answered no. I was encouraged by that. I have learned and changed and grown in each of my relationships, and I do not feel remorse.

I have felt keenly the judgment of others, however. Others reading this book might think that I should have seen that disaster was ahead, that I did not think through some of my choices well enough. Sometimes, perhaps, I should have accomplished more. I write because I want to be understood and accepted and known. I want others to appreciate the struggles I have endured and to be aware that life can be challenging when it hands a person a smorgasbord of experiences and events.

In the final analysis, I really have to write for myself so I can appreciate all that I have accomplished. When I was in the middle of a relationship with a troubled person, I learned a great deal about mental illness and addiction. I am tenacious and have been passionate about the people with whom I have shared my life.

I am sorry if my sons have suffered any shame stemming from my activities. I hope that my writing will not bring shame upon them. I haven't enjoyed the safety and security of a long-term, committed relationship. I thought I had that with their father. Still, I'm glad that they found life partners and have established happy and satisfying families.

As we look forward to the year of 2013, I think we should celebrate the 50 years of family their father and I began on July 2, 1963. There is a community hall at Brownfield. Many funerals are held there. It is large, and the community is well organized. When I go there for a wedding dance, very few people get up and dance. If I had a party celebrating 50 years of our family, I would certainly want to dance at it. I lost that feeling of belonging to a community when I lost Dave. I'm afraid that no one will come help me celebrate my family.

I am well familiar with the stigma associated with mental illness and suicide. My hope is that others will be relieved to know that someone else has endured bad experiences and learned to deal with them. I hope that people will feel better for knowing my story and about my struggles. I hereby invite them to feel compassion for me, as I am trying to have compassion for myself while on this journey through life.

I was drawn to Native people when I learned, at the first suicide prevention workshop I attended, that suicidal behaviours and suicide completions occur at higher rates among the Native population than among non-Native peoples. I often felt the stigma of suicide and mental illness, and so I continued to study and enquire. I had questions all my life. I went to Native people and felt sure that we shared feelings and experiences. My feeling of belonging to a community was ruptured by death, suicide and mental illness.

I was open and ready to go to Native people and share in our shame and sorrow. I thought we could understand each other's feelings. I could certainly identify with the trauma they dealt with. I would find that the sweat lodge, round dance and powwow were some of the ways these peoples came together to heal. Their funerals included three days of coming together to heal from their loss. I was ready and willing to help them and myself in our grief and loss.

I had a need to understand. I read many self-help books as well as 12-step program and addiction-themed books. I attended meetings and support groups. I liked the places we could sit in a circle and support each other with our eyes as we shared our stories. I went to so many workshops that I started to say that I wouldn't go to another one unless I was the instructor or facilitator. I might read a historical novel, but I rarely read fiction. Today, I read with a book club and enjoy discussing the works with other people. I look for memoirs because I like the honesty I find in them. I also like true stories describing lives lived by real people. I can appreciate fiction writers who can communicate complicated life experiences and make characters real and believable.

Hurting Again

I was preparing food for Thanksgiving with Dave's family, which has gathered together on this holiday every year for nearly 50 years. All of Dave's siblings and their spouses, children and grandchildren come to Doris's and Louis's Quonset hut close to Hardisty, near the original family farm.

Seven siblings of my late husband gathered together for a photo. *They are getting old,* I thought. I'm sure they felt honoured to be recognized by the younger generations. I told a younger person, one who had married into the family, that I had been married to Dave and that he had passed away many years ago. I got the impression that the young man didn't need any reminder.

I was among the people taking pictures with a digital camera. I took several photos; it was hard getting all of those people into one picture. I helped rearrange them away from the bright light of the Quonset door's windows.

Before I knew it, the spouses joined the group, and I was moving and snapping to make sure I had them all in the frame. I sat down to assess the situation and think. Martin didn't have a wife, and Allan had remarried after his wife died. My family wasn't represented. Dave's family wasn't in the picture! I should have been in that picture with the siblings and spouses.

I looked over and saw Sherri. Would I hand her my camera and get into the picture? For the sake of my grandchildren, I should be in that picture. Where do we all belong? What is my children's and my grandchildren's ancestry? Aren't they part of this big family that has been meeting this way for 49 years?

I wanted to be in the picture with my sisters and brothers-in-law. They thought that I had fully recovered from their brother's death and so didn't want to bring it up again. I thought that my grandchildren should see that I am part of the family. They are descendents and part of this big family reunion. I wanted to belong with my sons and their families. I felt slighted, forgotten, snubbed and pushed aside.

I said nothing. Then I was overcome. I sat frozen for a moment, holding back the tears. I bolted for the small door beside the big door. The big one had been open before someone closed it to make a better backdrop for the picture. I dodged around people and found my way to my car. My legs didn't work so well. Earlier, I had been able to park near the Quonset hut because I arrived early. I didn't want to be a straggler on this day.

I got into my car. Some of my sons' cousins were oblivious to the photo-taking and to my presence. They were visiting, driving trucks and leaning on my car. I cried so hard that I didn't think I could go back in. Inside, I had left my dishes from my salad and my squares. I went to the outdoor toilet, the Porta Potty, and tried to straighten myself out.

I could get through the door and get my things. I saw everyone else was lining up for supper. The door was crowded. I went back to my car and waited for a while longer. I wiped my eyes, blew my nose and looked into the mirror. I could see Tyler talking to someone. He and his family left while I was in the car. I guess he couldn't find me. Later, he told me that he had forgotten I was there or else he would have found me to say goodbye.

I was left out of the family picture. I do belong somewhere. I belong to no one. I have to be my own person.

The Body Hurts

The leaves crunch under my numb feet. These feet tell me that I have nowhere to go. Someone said that all of us have to get our story out so we can continue our lives. I am here where my story lives. I have run away before, so I guess there is nowhere left for me to go. I will keep writing or else run away again—either run from creeping paralysis or write until the numbness is gone. Is this how I numb the emotional pain resulting from my losses?

I have to get away from the critical thoughts that grind my joints. I have to forgive myself for not being good enough. I will forgive myself for all the lessons I have chosen to learn. I will celebrate the experiences and people I have brought into my life.

My three whiplash accidents caused the numbness I was feeling when I first returned to Coronation. I tripped and fell forward a few times when I was still living in Calgary. One day, I felt lucky when I fell up, instead of down, the steps of City Hall. I had also tripped and fallen on my elbow on a busy downtown street when I was walking to the courthouse to attend the trial of Gail Foley's murderer. That time, I had gone to the clinic at Eighth and Eighth to get stitches.

In Coronation, I would be walking to the post office and fall right down. I thought I was walking too fast because I had been in the walking program. I finally saw a doctor who referred me to a neurosurgeon in Calgary. The bones in my spine were impinging on my spinal cord and interfering with nerve impulses. I was losing feeling in my legs. The neurosurgeon preformed two surgeries in '04 and '07 on my back at the Foothills Hospital in Calgary.

My hips were bothering me so much that I had to move out of my townhouse. The laundry and bedrooms were on the lower floor. The stairs were painful for me to negotiate. In time, I would need a walker. I was referred to an orthopaedic surgeon in Medicine Hat. When he saw my X-rays, he told me that I needed both hips replaced and that he could perform the two surgeries five months apart from one another. I had a wheelchair ramp installed in the mobile home I bought, which stands two doors to the west of my townhouse. My hips would give out on me, so I started using a walker.

On January 21, 2010, I changed my surgery date to September 8 from March 24 because the treatments I started on September 22, 2009, seemed to be working in my favour. The start date for my treatments just happened to be my sister Julia's birthday. She phoned me on January 20, 2010, and was glad to hear of my progress.

Julia was on her way to another Habitat for Humanity build, this one in Guatemala. She told me that she'd contacted our old schoolmate Jim who leaves Nova Scotia to winter in Belize. She booked a five-day trip to his usual destination. Jim was my friend when I lived in Castor as an adult. Julia hadn't had the same chance to connect with him. *While with him,* I thought, *Julia will visit the past and also get a look into the future.*

I think it was Julia who told me that Jan's brother was contacted in Haiti after the earthquake and was found to be physically okay but, sure enough, experiencing emotional turmoil. I felt real concern for everyone in

Haiti because I had a holiday in the Dominican Republic in '03 and had wanted to visit the other half of the island, but I was discouraged on account of Haiti's poverty. The early slave revolt that established Haiti is so important to Haiti's people and to me. As a political animal, I am rooting for the Haitian people's successful future.

Travelling Back in Time

I went to Castor Ski Hill to witness my son Lee's first experience skiing on his new hip. He had his left hip replacement surgery in Calgary in December 2008.

It was a trip back in time and a glimpse into a healthier future, when I myself can have a new hip and enjoy more mobility. The fog added a surreal quality. I'd postponed my hip surgery to September because the treatments I was getting will have had a year to prove themselves— and maybe it would turn out that I could completely avoid the surgery. I'd already seen progress.

As I drove Highway 12 between Coronation and the Highway 36 junction in the fog, I passed the place where I had been hit from behind during a blizzard in 1992. I reminded myself that when visibility is poor, I have to beware of letting cars overtake and pass me, and I have to be aware of those vehicles I may want to pass. After all my car accidents, I've learned that on the highway of life I have to look ahead and anticipate consequences. Since doing that, I've had more positive outcomes—touch wood, I haven't even had a fender-bender.

As I drove farther, I saw South Beaver Road and North Beaver Road. The Strome family lived at Beaver. When we were young, we came here to look for and pick Saskatoon berries. I don't know if we were anywhere near the old home at the time.

I had been in another accident when I was teaching at Brownfield, but I wasn't the driver that time. Before this highway was built, I was travelling with a friend from Alliance in a car without brakes. We were heading south down the hill beside the Coppick farm and were going too fast for the driver to negotiate the corner. The car rolled into the ditch. One of the first things we found strewn about the car was the ketchup bottle we'd taken when we had gotten hamburgers in Alliance.

My friends and I had visited with Gwen Coppick while we waited for a more reliable car and driver to pick us up. That was the night I lost my virginity—and when *I* should have hit the brakes. It happened on the ground at the north side of the house. Our impatient driver was honking the horn. My parents were supposed to be asleep.

I was returning to this ski hill where my sons and I had learned to ski in the seventies. Joan and her boys had left their equipment for us when they had moved to Dallas.

Lee was skiing for the first time on his new left hip, as I mentioned, which had been replaced a year prior. Nate and Sydney, almost 4 and almost 5, respectively, got free lift passes because they hadn't had their birthdays yet. It was a joy for me to see them outfitted and on their skis for the very first time. I was out there on the snow with my cane helping them with their first steps. I overdid it a bit, but it was worth it to go back inside the lodge and watch them be helped up the tow rope and then crouch on their hands on knees and slide down the hill. Lee's hip stood the test. I thought he'd have to stop before little Nate got enough. The little guy, at 45 pounds, is heavier and wears a larger shoe size than his sister, who is older than he is by a little more than a year. They both had a marvellous first ski.

On the way home, I went to see Hazel (Mom). Her mobile home sits on the old path that used to lead to the well where my sisters and I would fetch water for drinking and other household uses.

Mom was standing at her table leafing through a Sears catalogue and didn't hear or see me on the deck. When I went in, she put in her hearing aid. We decided to have supper at the Shangri-La in Castor so we'd have more time to visit. She was excited about seeing the pictures of Julia's grandson Sam.

Mom and I verify family history when we get together, and I'm so happy to spend time with her. I am lucky to have her in my life after all these years.

I borrowed Mom's copy of my uncle William Annett's book *Called to Preach*. I struggle to understand my evangelical roots and respect the religious motivations of my mother's family. The conflict shows itself in my father's life and in his only brother's life as well. My father turned away from

211

my mother's religion. His brother married my mother's cousin and embraced Mennonite theology to become a lifelong preacher of the gospel.

Jan and Harley have a special place in my story. Growing up, I knew when Jan and her twin brother, James, were born to my mother's cousin.

One of our family reunions was held at Jan's brother's home near Red Deer. My brother Harley had been divorced for many years. Jan was newly widowed and was living near Hanna. Jan is a granddaughter to Great-Uncle Wilmot Wideman, and Harley is a grandson of my grandfather Sam Annett. His mother is a Strome. He and Jan both loved farming. My sister and I were suggesting another Wideman and Annett marriage. I talked to Jan while Julia talked to Harley. They married on Vancouver Island in 2008.

Harley still has some cattle and responsibilities on the farm we had grown up on. Mom still lives there, so he does a good job of looking out for her and keeping in touch by phone. My brother Patric and his wife, Barb, are four miles away. Jan and Harley have 70 or 80 goats that give birth to their kids every spring at the farm at Scapa.

Coming Home to Faith

I had a crisis of faith this morning. I cried last night and knew I just couldn't go to church and cry all the way through the service. I'm so full of words. I can't sit and listen to how perfect God's love is while I am feeling unworthy. My words are flooding me. I can't control the sadness.

I went away after the deaths of my first two husbands. I was absorbed in my marriages and my family, but without a partner I felt compelled to run away from my feelings. The times I felt at home in a church were when I attended 12-step-program meetings. I even walked in the back door of this selfsame United Church to go to meetings in the basement.

I've come home to people who don't know all the life I've lived outside this rural community. I had dreams and was excited when I found myself as a grief support worker and educator, as a group facilitator, as a wife again (and stepmother and foster mother) and as an adult Native upgrading instructor. My dreams didn't endure. My optimism faded and I couldn't sustain the excitement. I put the pieces of my life together, but I still felt I hadn't achieved enough.

I had experienced another bit of excitement, another burst of optimism, when I was 16 and was saved at Gull Lake Bible Camp. I was in university when I told my uncle Willie that I couldn't sustain the excitement and emotion connected to my evangelical redemption.

Now, when I open up my throat to sing, I can no longer hold back my feelings. This is something that has carried over from my youth and into my adult life. Some of the songs I hear today were sung during altar call when I was a youth, when the evangelicals wanted us to go to the front of the church and be saved.

The more experienced girls would say, "Don't blow your nose. They'll try to take you to the front."

They sang "Softly and Tenderly, Jesus Is Calling" that evening when I was 16. My guard had been down, as this was a song I played and sang at home, enjoying it on our piano. I went up to the altar to be saved, and as a result there was much rejoicing among the camp leaders that night.

One Sunday we sang an old hymn that I've loved all my life. I played the melody of the hymn with my right hand (and ignored my left hand) to accompany my singing. The hymn was "Will Your Anchor Hold in the Storms of Life?"

I cried all the way through this hymn that I love. My anchor wasn't holding. I tried to relate to the nautical theme. I tried to concentrate and listen to my voice. Emotion overcame me. The tears ran down. My throat was choked and I could not sing. I lost my childhood reassurance of faith when my first husband died.

My mood on this day was one of anger and resentment. I was resentful that women in this church and congregation had enjoyed many more years of marriage than I had.

I was experiencing crying spells and was feeling sad. The winter, my diminished mobility, my trouble going to church, and my dealing with my losses was more than I can handle. I am being honest about how I feel regarding these occurrences in my life. The writing does trigger my emotions, but I can write it down and then walk away, resuming doing the things I need to do to maintain my house and life.

I didn't leave my house for the entire weekend, as I was involved with introspection, thinking about the sadness that prevents me from enjoying my church community. Church, for me, is a place of contemplation where feelings that are hard to name rise up. I recall funerals where I was too much in shock to cry. When I think back on my marriage ceremonies, I recall bright anticipation that leads to happiness and then great loss.

I'm writing about all the matters that crowd into my mind and make me feel angry, resentful, sad, guilty, hurt, lost and unloved.

The day finally came when the church continued its series about honouring God's creation. Reverend Sue brought photos of mountains, and I was reminded of our family, our three cousins and our mountain—the Three Sisters at Canmore. I was looking through the psalms and found number 121: "I will lift up my eyes to the hills—from whence cometh my help?" Years ago, I had asked that it be read at Dave's funeral, and I also included it in one of my scrapbooks:

Psalm 121

I lift up my eyes to the hills—
from where will my help come?
My help comes from the Lord,
who made heaven and earth.
He will not let your foot be moved:
he who keeps you will not slumber.
He who keeps Israel
will neither slumber nor sleep.
The Lord is your keeper;
the Lord is your shade at your right hand.
The sun shall not strike you by day,
nor the moon by night.
The Lord will keep you from all evil;
he will keep your life.
The Lord will keep
your going out and your coming in
from this time and
forevermore.

We sang some of my favourite hymns, such as "Morning Has Broken" and "For the Beauty of the Earth." Sue called her reflection "Mountain Sunday." Then we sang "God of the Sparrow." One of its lyrics—"God of the prodigal"—still speaks to me. I have to have compassion for myself. Perhaps I am not the one who wasted my riches, but the one who returns after an absence. I do feel guilty about misusing the money and property my first husband had left me. My next two marriages were not as financially productive as the first. The last line of the hymn is, "God of the loving heart/How do your children say Joy/How do your children say *Home.*"

There has now been a change in my ability to enjoy church services. My process of being honest about my feelings and writing my story has relieved the strong emotions that attending church used to arouse in me. I feel cared for by the community that is our church. I think that having a female minister helps me, also, as I don't perceive a judgmental "father figure" on the altar to remind me of God the Father. It's nice, too, that the coffee has been moved upstairs, onto the two tables behind the pews.

One of my favourite hymns speaks of my connection to nature and the weather. One line of it goes, "He hideth my soul in the cleft of a rock that shadows a dry, thirsty land."

I put the television on mute while I listen to Eric Clapton's "Living on Tulsa Time," but I still looked at the screen, which showed a caption reading, "Africa, 1914." A herd of horses was being driven and forced to swim in the ocean, and then driven onto land and herded into corrals. A big grey horse broke away from the men and the rest of the herd. It looked out into the ocean before it was caught and returned to the others. Another horse was still struggling in the water. It managed to beat the waves and come ashore. This one was a colt. It was chased into the corrals, where the horses were then given water. The colt was still trying to reach its mother while the mother was calling to it. They were all driven onto a train to travel across the desert, a desert with shifting sand dunes.

I turned off the show to continue listening to Eric Clapton: "Tell me that you love me." And I was left with the image of the colt trying to find its mother.

I thought to myself that the practice of modern medicine is threatening to rob my readers of learning of my story. I am some years into the writing process, and I no longer wake early, squirming in pain until I have to leave my bed. I can now remain lying down and get some extra hours of sleep, falling back into my dreams. I arise to summer light, and I check my garden before I make my coffee.

This morning, I spent three hours playing Spider Solitaire instead of writing. I see this as a sign of depression. I am wasting my senior years instead of wasting away my youth.

I justify my excesses because I had deprived myself for so long. Previously, solitaire was elusive to me. I had only played it at Medicine Hat on my son's computer because I couldn't find it on mine. Now I have it available all the time. I've won some games and have found playing to be relaxing and challenging, but it is becoming addictive. When I play cards at the drop-in, and also when I play solitaire at home, I see each new hand or game as an opportunity. I hold the hope that with this new one, I will play better than the last time. I recall the optimism I felt when I started a new relationship. I didn't know what pitfalls to look for. I always wanted to be needed and useful, but I wasn't clear about what *I* needed.

Rebuilding

I have a compost pile in the back corner of my yard. There, I put down all the corrugated sheets of cardboard that once held my office furniture. Then I piled branches from the shrubs I had pruned. I added compost and sand. I planted the three sisters of Native tradition: corn, squash and beans. This is the third year I've done so.

One spring day, I climbed up the steep north face of the butte on the ranch. I could use my arms and legs to aid me in my ascent to the summit. It might have been the spring after I had returned to Coronation in fall of 2002. I wanted to perform a ceremony to affirm our need for rain in the coming summer. I carried my smudge bowl, sweet grass and sage, and matches in my shoulder bag. When I was looking for rocks for the four directions, I found one that had lichen on it.

As I walked around on the summit, I learned that that rock had been kicked out of an ancient medicine ring of four stones. I had my small camera with me and took pictures of the valley, river and oxbow. This high point offered a panorama view of the open river valley and the hills that pastured our herd of cattle. I photographed north, east, south and west.

Here I share with you another poem I wrote that tells of my personal journey:

Ebb and Flow

The rise and fall,
The ebb and flow,
Power, life, creation,
Sadness and joy.
The plant that bursts forth from the ground
Flowers and dies.
Weakness and strength,
Up and down,
Energy and tiredness.
A house torn down,
Another raised from the earth.

Lavera Goodeye, 2003

My moods can change so quickly. I was happy to be with my birth mother when she was still alive, but many of the pictures of me as a child show me frowning in the sun when my sisters are laughing. I loved the dances and outings I attended when I was a teenager, but my dad thought I misbehaved at them. Later in life, the men I liked would move on or leave me. Two of my husbands died. I was disillusioned when the addictions of my second and third husband proved to be so entrenched. I had envisioned a glorious future, our sons growing and succeeding on our ranch, but it had all changed so fast. When I am happy and joyful, I fearfully await a crash, for sadness to come again and sit on my shoulders.

I am alone but don't name my feeling as loneliness. It is more. I am the lost little girl looking for her mother. Bob was a little boy who was lost. Did I see my mother when I looked into his eyes?

My first impression of Bob was not of a little boy lost, but he did eventually tug at my heart. My response to him had its roots in my own beginnings as a lost little girl. I was that pathetic little girl who had lost her mother and was kept out of school for a year so she could start later with her sister. Was my mother already dead in her own mind? Did she want me to be home with her?

Seventy

When I realized I would turn 70 on Friday the 13th of November, I made plans. The Canadian Finals Rodeo (CFR) usually falls on my birthday, so I could forget about getting my family together to celebrate. Dave, my first husband, never went to the CFR. We had gone to an indoor rodeo in Red Deer two days before he died. At that rodeo, it was announced that the first CFR would be held that fall. In the year of my 70th birthday, my grandsons were competing in their events. Clay was among the top 10 money winners in the Saddle Bronc category, and Luke was among the top 10 in Bareback. I phoned my youngest son, Tyler, to see if I could buy tickets for the two of us. He has a sister-in-law who lives in Fort Saskatchewan. He could stay there, and his wife and daughters could visit.

I got tickets for Saturday afternoon and evening. On Friday the 13th, I drove very carefully, using the less travelled highways. I didn't want to have an accident. I had reservations for two nights at a Fort Saskatchewan hotel. There was a Western wear store at a shopping mall nearby, so I bought two Western shirts for myself.

I picked up Tyler in the morning, and we drove to the coliseum called Rexall Place. I know that I enjoyed seeing Clay and Luke ride their bucking horses. My body would strain as I watched the intense action. They spurred the horses and responded to their movements. I was having trouble getting up and down the stairs and so had brought my walker with me. I was in the handicapped people's seating area for some of the time.

Between the two shows, we went on the overpass across 18th Avenue to attend the farm show. Cattle were tied up in stalls, where their handlers would curry and groom them before leading them to the ring to be judged. Two more of my sons and their families found us there. Colin got in the line-up for mini-donuts and bought some for all of us. Kelly and Sandy were checking out the cookware and boots for Cassidy. We also got in the line for barbecued beef and beans. There were so many people that it was hard to find a place to sit with our plates. When it was time for the evening performance, we walked back to the coliseum together.

Mental Health Training

On a Tuesday and a Wednesday, I got up early and went to Castor to attend mental health first-aid training. I've experienced a lifetime of mental health problems. The training described mental health conditions or events that required intervention to save a young person from committing suicide. It also stressed the need to direct people to the resources available to help them get better.

There are so many different classifications. I appreciated learning more about something of which I thought I already had extensive firsthand knowledge. When addiction was the topic, I got a better understanding of the progressive nature of the condition. The person who has an addiction needs more and more of the pill or drug to get the same effect. I myself have used addictive painkillers, but I always followed doctors' orders and never increased the dosage.

On the second day of training, I had a physical reaction to the material. I was dizzy and nauseous, experiencing a flashback to the insanity of Bob's life and suicide. Elements of post-traumatic stress disorder were apparent in me.

I recognized the importance of bringing mental health services to this rural area. I was reminded of the project some of us did for the Canadian Mental Health Association. A number of us rural women told about how we tried to deal with the issues we faced. We produced a booklet, *Through the Eyes of Women.* My story was called "Widowhood and Stigma."

On the evening after our workshop, Paintearth County was celebrating 50 years. Our Golden Age Group was selling copies of the *Coronation History Book.* I enjoyed the evening, as I was surrounded by our members— and we sold six books. I talked to a number of people, including a Beebe family member who used to provide music for the dances of my youth.

The wife of our current county reeve works on my old acreage for the Battle River Convention Centre. Pat Fredrick, the fellow who had bought the property and established the Convention Centre, had requested a picture of the house that had burned down. My internal response to this request was more intense than most anyone would think reasonable. I felt that he wanted to steal my past from me. That land and my experiences on it go much deeper than a mere picture can illuminate. The picture represents a whole chunk of my life. It was as if letting him use the picture would tear that part of my life from my body.

When I was reading the mental health manual the day after the workshop and the anniversary celebration, a whole lot of memories came rushing back to me. I had to use a tool I had used in the past. I got out the lined paper I had left from taking notes, and I wrote out the thoughts that flooded my mind.

I used to call the product of this type of writing my "yucky checklist." When I was feeling bad but didn't know why, I would write out my thoughts and, from there, determine which experience had hurt me the most. After writing and reviewing my thoughts now, I determined that I felt poorly because the mental health first-aid course had made fresh in my mind a lot of my firsthand experiences with mental illness.

I had called for a lot of help when Bob was suicidal. Even though he had talked to his mother before he killed himself, none of us has been able to stop him. My friend had saved my life by taking me away to the 12-step roundup in Medicine Hat.

I realized that the two-day workshop had taken a toll on me. I wondered what I could do to feel better and decided that I might go out to the acreage. The largest concern in my mind was Bob's suicide and how we had all been so helpless when it came to doing what needed to be done. My crying felt out of control. I felt helpless and hopeless.

I decided to have a shower. *No, I'll run a bath,* I thought.

The bath did calm me.

I had to find my way out of the negative thoughts that were overwhelming me. After my lunch, I went to bed for the whole afternoon. I called it a mental health day.

When I awoke in late afternoon, I thought I might mow the lawn. I was feeling weak and shaky, so instead I turned on the air conditioning and went outside to read a book about gardening and acreage living.

My house was cooler when I went inside. I didn't mow the lawn. It was better to take it easy and know that taking a mental health day is something I can do when I become overwhelmed by emotion.

The workshop had triggered an episode of anxiety, however. I did have flashbacks of earlier experiences. The training emphasized my need to hold myself together, especially given my fear that I, like my birth mother, was mentally ill.

When my first husband died, I was sure I didn't have the strength I needed to endure the life of a single widowed parent. At the time, if I received a sympathy card containing the word *strong,* I felt a compulsion to pull the word off the page. Another of my fears when I was first widowed was that I would turn to alcohol and neglect my children.

As I play Spider Solitaire, I think of my writing and how I am beginning to accept my life's journey. When the cards fall into place and I win, I think of the events of my life and how the pieces fall into place in a finished, complete whole.

I found a sympathy card I had bought but never sent. When I read it, I realized that it wouldn't have been very helpful to someone who had experienced a recent loss. When I found it in the drugstore, though, it spoke directly to my history.

> Without sorrow,
> The heart would never learn
> The meaning of joy.
>
> Without tears,
> Our eyes would never see
> What we hold inside.
>
> Without darkness,
> We would have no reason
> To look to the light of heaven.
>
> —Irish Proverb

My mental health journey has compelled me to look for a high level of self-awareness. I have had to do a lot of journaling and processing as a result. I learned that I have been holding on so tightly ever since I was a little girl. My toes are curled under from the effort I have put forth.

It seems that I designed my own recovery and survival program. I didn't have a professional to help me with it. When the pupil is ready, the teacher will appear, they say. My consultants and the resources I used are many and varied. I'm now able to see the opportunities I faced on my pathway, and I also notice that I found help at every turn. Perhaps my mother has been guiding from her place among the chosen. My life shows evidence of the Creator's hand at work. I have been divinely guided even though I didn't pray for it. Sometimes I believe that my relatives were praying for me.

The song at church this past Sunday brought it to light for me: "I Was There to Hear Your Borning Cry."

The memory of my mother, which I have carried so faithfully, has sustained me. Also, my belief that I can write out these pages has carried me forward.

Changing Seasons

A few days after that Sunday at church, I stepped outside and found my gloves where I had left them after my last round of weeding. There was a fresh new smell in the air. Was it autumn coming on, as indicated by the yellow leaves tumbling off my neighbour's maple tree? As I pulled weeds, I speculated that the smell was the rain coming.

Drops dotted the sidewalk, but I kept finding weeds and pulling them. I had to dig out the Canada thistle and the dandelion. Some weeds broke off at the root, so I dug with my fingers to find them and pull them out. I bent from my hips, resting my right hand on my right knee and pulling with my left. I don't kneel on my garden kneeling bench because there isn't room for me, what with all my volunteer bachelor buttons and calendula. I try not to step on the petunias and groundcover.

When the rain became more substantial, I threw the last handful of weeds into the tub and left the garden. When I got to my door, I looked across the back alley and saw that the vacant lots' grass had been cut for the first time this summer. There was a lot of alfalfa. The fresh-cut hay was what I had smelled when I had stepped outside.

Later that year, I came out to a shiny layer of brilliant yellow leaves from our tame northwest poplars. These leaves flow like water over my gravel parking lot, all around and onto my car. These leaves come from my neighbour's trees. Within the space of a few days, the golden blanket turned to tan and became rumpled. The leaves had dried, so now the wind could catch them and shuffle them into piles. The leaves were the size of the palm of my hand. A larger leaf arrived from a distant tree. It was three times as large—the size of my outstretched hand. I looked around but couldn't see any tree bearing this large a leaf.

The quaking aspens that grow wild in the fields have much smaller leaves, the size of a loonie (our Canadian dollar). These aspens grow in rounded groves and are dying of old age. Our tame poplars also die after 40 years if they aren't pruned of deadwood.

The drive along the north side of the Nose Hills is delightful. Many shrubs, berry bushes, willows and buckbrush have lost their leaves and turned purple. Poplars are still golden, and the harvested fields are tan. Sloughs bear weeds and plants that have turned to shades of rust and mahogany. The foxtail flowers are fluffy and blond. This carpet of colours flows over the hills and gullies and all along the roads. The sky was still light when a huge full moon slid from behind a cloud.

I enjoy the pastel colours of winter. The mauve, pink and coral of sunset reflect onto the snow, whereupon I see all the shades of blue. Driving south to Hanna at noon to celebrate Christmas with my four sons and their families, I saw the rosy hues of sunset along the horizon. The sky was aqua blue. On other days, the sun might be a splinter of pale yellow breaking though grey-clouded skies.

This morning, the blazing reds and oranges of sunrise filled my kitchen window.

My mornings are so different now. The days where I'd feel pain and take medication are long gone. In winter, I can stay in bed until the morning light welcomes me. I like the way my home is situated. My bathroom is all the way across the north end of my 16-foot-wide trailer. It has a window above its two-sink counter. In the east, clear plastic cubes above the corner Jacuzzi tub let in the morning light. A French door and some interior plastic allow light from the sunrise to filter into my bedroom. More morning light floods in from my kitchen.

The dining table and china cabinet are on the east wall. Kitchen cabinets and appliances have a generous skylight above them. A leafy plant spreads on the divider between the kitchen and living room.

My living room has a large west window featuring fake leaded windows (grills between the panes) and a dormer. Before I bought this home, I made sure that my patchwork curtains from my last home would fit the windows. The wall between the kitchen and living room is filled with bookcases. My seating includes a moss green chair, a chesterfield and a round red chair.

I found a cabinet that accommodates my photo scrapbooks and my television. I bought the perfect oval-glass-topped coffee table for the centre of my room, too. I chose it because of its traditional style and also because it matches the curving lines of the soft furniture and the TV cabinet. My curtain rods and lamps are also traditional.

I made the east wall into a gallery, with pictures above and around the black-framed television and lining the wall that reaches all the way to my dining table. One item I still have is a stained glass curio cabinet that Bob had made. There is a space for my repaired clock.

Photos of my grandchildren are switched out when new ones arrive. I have Native paintings and pen-and-ink drawings. I bought two East Indian batiks depicting rural activities. They grace the wall above my chesterfield.

The Men in My Life

I was watching Dr. Phil again. He often tells fathers of teenage daughters how important their relationship is. This allows me to reflect: I do see that my father did come through for me by encouraging my education and not comparing my report card to Joan's. He helped me get through the first summer after Dave died by taking my boys and me to Ontario to get the school bus and taking us to Naramata. When I first started dating, he asked me to tell him about the boys I was seeing. I was glad for his interest. Other times, he would tell Joan that he didn't like my choice of hairdressing as a career, or he would say that a truck driver wasn't a good choice for a boyfriend. He didn't say these things to me, however. He told Joan, and then she would tell me. That is how he influenced my choices. I didn't become a hairdresser and I didn't marry a truck driver.

I read *The Painted Veil* by W. Somerset Maugham and was struck by it, as it reminded me that sometimes I fail to see the full dimensions of the men in my life. The character Lily hadn't realized that her husband, Walter, had a soft and tender side, one that allowed him to hold and nurture a tiny baby. She had been taken in by the man who told her how beautiful she was and then seduced her. She was pregnant, likely by the other man she had been with, and her husband died of cholera before her baby was born. She later came to appreciate her father. From this, I saw that I often assign men the provider role and then take them for granted.

I can look to my past in order to learn lessons from it—and then use those lessons to enhance my present. My writing has granted me a large measure of insight into, healing from and acceptance of my choices. I am reminded of Bob's creative work in designing and building the house. It was as if he had been putting himself together as he incorporated roof lines, chimneys and all the various other trade work into his masterpiece. On one of his diagrams of brick arches is the handwritten note, "And we can so order life."

Sometimes I needed to be needed. When I went willingly into the trenches, I got more than I had bargained for. I still use readings from 12 step books to help me be grateful for all the sustaining support I have received in the basements of churches in Calgary, Coronation and Valleyview. These programs have helped me to heal.

Dave lives on in my sons and their families and me because he was a provider. The ranch sustained our young family and me, and the land still sustains me. Dave was a figure of industry and integrity. His gravestone reads, "Life's Work Well Done." My two oldest sons share his passion for working with animals and ranching. They and their families enjoy living close to the land. I experience healing and strength when my feet feel the earth.

Sweet Sadness

Parting is such sweet sadness.
It lays heavy on my being.
Happiness shared will remain,
Full of meaning as complete
As a cloud ready to fall as rain,
Drinking the cup to its very dregs.
One does not know sorrow in its full dimensions
Until experiencing the leave-taking that comes
With a loved one's death,
Sweetened by memories tenderly held.

Lavera Goodeye, 1989

The Value of Family

I went to Hanna for a night and a day. My youngest son, Tyler, and his wife were volunteering at a casino in Red Deer. The funds raised were to be used for the gymnastics club their daughter Amanda attended. Sarah, who is 11, had tae kwon do lessons from 8:00 to 9:00 p.m., while Amanda had a bedtime of 8:30. Sarah knew that her sister would be lonesome for her parents, so I went back to help Amanda into bed. On her bed, I found the smiling octopus and happy stars on the baby quilt I had made for her.

I borrowed Laura's copy of *Relationship Rescue,* written by Dr. Phil. Maybe I could find out where I went right and then honour myself for surviving many relationships.

If I can see past the pain and trauma and loss, then maybe I can see my accomplishments. My sister Joan's three sons valued education; my sons saw finding and then caring for life partners as important. I can review the special moments I have with my adult sons and their partners and know that family is paramount. Sometimes in the past, my loneliness sent me into the arms of another man. My sons were hurt by my relationship choices.

My life and my partners did influence my sons. Tyler was growing up during those seven years when Bob struggled to make a four-sided planer to cut into raw lumber so he could fashion tongue-and-groove cedar siding or white oak crown moulding. He was there when Bob formed angle iron and pillow blocks and pulleys and shafts into machinery that would grind quarter-inch glass to make a bevelled glass window. He was there when Bob used an ancient dowel machine to drill the hole that would accommodate the crosspiece to make an old-fashioned stile-and-rail door.

I was there, too, making my blundering way through hurtful relationships, while my sons intuitively knew whom they wanted to marry and establish a family with. I was struggling to find a new career when they were progressing through their educations and finding job opportunities that suited their skills.

When Tyler and Laura returned from Red Deer, Tyler was unpacking the tools he bought for his trade as a millwright at the power plant. Bob had consulted a machinist or a millwright when he was building his bevelling equipment.

When Bob was growing up as the oldest of five boys, his father was working in a wallpaper factory, likely as a machinery maintenance worker. He left that job to take on contract work involving all kinds of trades so he could work with his sons and teach them those skills.

The family even bought a water-powered mill that produced barrel staves. They hoped to restore it to show how wood was milled in the days before electricity. Bob and I went with his brother and father to visit that mill beside a swift flowing stream.

My sons didn't have their father, but their uncles were their best resources. From them, they learned what Dave would have taught them about animal husbandry and farming.

I needed strength and determination to survive all I have experienced, and I am pleased to see these qualities in my sons, too. They have endured and thrived and are effective in the work they have chosen. They have learned and studied. They are capable, loving, nurturing parents.

As a politician, ranch and farm wife, teacher, social worker, grief support worker, businesswoman and writer, my greatest accomplishment is my family. My sons and their wives have learned what it takes to establish stable families, and they continue working to maintain those families. They are teaching their children the skills and values they will take into their adult lives. There have been hard knocks and disappointments along the way, but they have persevered.

They have beautiful, intelligent children. The sisters Sarah and Amanda have grown out of their fighting and pouting and blaming phases. Now they are playful and loving together.

Lee has a boy and girl who are close in age, like Joan and I were. They have their fights, but they are good company for each other. Lee is the only one with three kids. His oldest is graduating from high school this year. They waited many hopeful and hopeless years for their second and—surprise, surprise—third child. Lee was my surprise pregnancy. I am sure that my sister Joan was a surprise to my parents, too. Joan has sons who are a year apart in age. Someone told me of the designation "Irish twins" for children born close together.

My granddaughters bring me joy as they learn to play the piano, clarinet or guitar, and as they do the "boy things" like bow hunting, shooting gophers and practicing tae kwon do. The girls outnumber the boys in my family.

We, my family and I, started out with the rodeo cowboys and ranch cowboys, Clay and Luke. The bouncy little girl with the head of reddish curls, Dallas, was next. A third family started with Garrett. He was a basketball player before he was 2. Now he is the one with curls, which he refuses to tame or cut. His sister Cassidy arrived on an October night. Kelly and his son and his daughter were all born on the same day of the month.

Then it was time for Laura and Tyler to start their family. There was disappointment along the way, but their first daughter, Sarah, was born the day before Laura's 30th birthday.

Amanda was another October baby, and she came to be Sarah's sister.

Dallas, Lee and Sherri's daughter, had to wait for her siblings, Sydney and Nate. Sydney asked for a guitar for Christmas. Nate is a cowboy through and through. He was excited to celebrate his 7th birthday at the 113th annual Calgary Bull Sale.

Members of my birth family and their mates and offspring gather for birthdays, family reunions and holidays. My two sisters live with their husbands in British Columbia, but their five sons live in Calgary. My brothers Sheldon, Patric and Harley, and their wives live in Alberta, so we can get together. Hazel (Mom) and I are single. Any number of people can play the card game 2,500 Rummy. The plus and minus amounts make for complicated scorekeeping, but Barb willingly handles this task.

Mom loves the flowers, perennials and shrubs she has collected and tended to for so many years. Harley works up her garden patch for her, where she produces many vegetables. Her fruit trees supply Jan's goats with special treats. I may enjoy an afternoon picking raspberries from her ample patch. She gives me the ones she picked herself, along with some carrots.

Another Easter

I brought home a hymnbook because I wanted to see the words of the hymn that has the line "Though ancient walls . . ." I thought what followed was "divide us." In any event, I knew that the words spoke of inequality and injustice. It had affected me deeply when I sang it.

The first verse goes like this: "Though ancient walls may stand proud/and racial strife be fact/though boundaries may be lines of hate,/proclaim God's saving act!"

Another line says this: "Unites us in a common quest for self and world made new."

This hymn was written before the Berlin Wall was taken down. I attended the Peace Conference in Halifax before that had happened. The wall was used to separate East Germany from West Germany, but it came to mean much more than that. This separation of communist Russia (the USSR) from the rest of the world eventually led Mennonites from colonies inside Russia to flee and come to Canada.

I have experienced religious differences in my life, and they have caused me to ponder the lessons in the Bible as well as those I've heard during church services. My country, Canada, is attempting to make amends to our Native people who have suffered from the residential school system that, in the name of religion, ripped apart the culture and structure of our First Nations.

"Yea, though I walk through the valley of the shadow of death, I will fear no evil." I walk this lonesome valley willingly and with courage. I feel I have this story to tell. This is a story of pain and loss. This is story of going into the depths of despair and then emerging from them. After my first husband died, I thought I was forced to drink the cup of life to its very dregs.

I have said that the Creator really loves me; just look at all the lessons he has sent my way. The love of my Creator shows in his protection of me and in my survival.

I put my family in grave danger. I lived my life under the shadow of suicide. I had all of those questions—for example, "Why did my mother leave without me?" When Bob was in the Philippines looking for another wife, I had this question for my father: "Why did my mother and I come back to the farm?" We were on the farm when she planned our suicide. I was in grave danger when I was a child. When Bob was suicidal, I was in danger because a person's urge to kill himself or herself often leads him or her to commit homicide, too.

I've had a willingness to go where others fear to tread. I, like the sand in the oyster shell, am an irritant that will not let go. I refuse to stop talking about the pain in my life. Can I see that God has created in me the pearl of great price? Am I capable of seeing that I have value?

I have been a fearless and calming influence in the lives of my children. I and my sons have had each other and the families they established, which has brought stability to our adult lives. I will look to the hills from whence cometh my help. I once feared God's retribution for the magic I tried to make in my life. I feared that the Christian God would punish me and strike me dead. Then I was reminded of the wisdom of creation: the earth grounds the electricity of lightning.

As I draw my story to its conclusion, I feel sadness when I think of Dave's death during that Easter season 40 years ago. I try to see my way through the tears. I ask him why he didn't stay with me to see our sons grow to men and become loving, happy husbands and fathers. He didn't stay to hold his granddaughters on his knee. He wasn't here to cheer on our cowboys or teach them how to rope. He wasn't here to put a hand on their shoulders and say, "You have accomplished much in your life, my son."

My Christmas cactus started blooming at the end of November, and it was still putting out new buds on the first day of spring. It is in full bloom again for Easter.

The Easter story is so entwined with my own story of grief over having lost my first husband, Dave. He died on Tuesday, a day when there was no school for my sons. Friday would be Good Friday, so his funeral was held on that Saturday. Every year, Easter and April are a sad time for me.

I wanted to attend all the church events and services to come to terms with what I saw as Jesus' willingness to go to his death. We had Bible study on Wednesday morning, and that was the first time I understood that the political climate of Jesus' time was such that the people in power saw him as a treat. They were trying to destroy his message and the meaning of his life. We read the part about Christ's praying to God, his Father, asking him to take the cup away from him. We read about Peter's denying that he knew Jesus three times before the rooster crowed.

On Thursday night, I read a part for the service. It was the saddest part of all—when the darkness falls, the earth shakes and Jesus dies.

I felt the sadness again at the Good Friday service when we sang, "Were you there when they crucified our Lord?" I wanted to hear the piano and sing the notes, "Oh, oh, oh, it causes me to tremble, tremble, tremble." If I had been at the piano, I would have played and sang them. I wasn't ever that good at playing songs with three flats.

The fragile red flowers of my Christmas cactus extend from the strands of green and cascade over the edges of the pot.

As I say goodbye to you, my reader, I hope that I shall hear your stories. I sit at my computer and watch the smoke curl from my smudge bowl to the feathered dream catcher pinned to my translucent curtain. Afternoon light filters in. Thank you.

Bibliography

Alcoholics Anonymous: Big Book, 4th edition. New York: Alcoholics Anonymous World Services, Inc., 2001.

Annett, Pastor William D. *Called to Preach.* Edmonton, Alberta: Eunoia Publishing, 2011.

Baldwin, Christina. *Storycatcher: Making Sense of Our Lives through the Power and Practice of Story.* Novato, CA: New World Library, 2005.

Boon, Clarence A. *I Was a Step-Child.* Brandon, Manitoba: Leech Printing, 1975.

Brewster, Eva. *Vanished in Darkness: An Auschwitz Memoir.* Edmonton, Alberta: NeWest Press, 1987.

Brown, Rosemary Margaret. *Rupture in the Ties That Bind,* master's thesis. University of Calgary © 1990. Ann Arbor, MI: University of Michigan Press, 1997.

Castor and District History Book Committee. *Beaver Tales from Castor and District.* Altona, Manitoba: Friesens Corporation, 2012.

Collins, Judy. *Singing Lessons*. New York: Pocket Books, 1998.

Kupfer, Lorraine. *Through the Eyes of Women*. Alberta South Central Region: Canadian Mental Health Association, 1990.

Maugham, Somerset W. *The Painted Veil*. New York: G. H. Doran, 1925.

McGraw, Phillip C., PhD. *Relationship Rescue: A Seven-Step Strategy for Reconnecting with Your Partner*. New York: Hyperion, 2000.

Old-Timer's Centennial Book Committee. *Shadows of the Neutrals: Open Memory's Door*. College Heights, Alberta: College Press, 1967.

Mrs. Barkis Reesor (Ida Wideman), compiled. *The Family Chain*. Markham County, Ontario: self published, 1931.

Regan, Paulette. *Unsettling the Settler Within: Indian Residential Schools, Truth Telling and Reconciliation in Canada*. Vancouver: University of British Columbia Press, 2010.

Rosenfeld, Linda, and Marilynne Prupas. *Left Alive: After a Suicide Death in the Family*. Springfield, IL: C. C. Thomas, 1984.

Toews, Miriam. *Swing Low: a life*. Toronto, Ontario: Stoddart, 2000.

United Church of Canada. *Voices United: The Hymn and Worship Book of the United Church of Canada.* Etobicoke, Ontario: United Church of Canada Press, 1996.

CPSIA information can be obtained
at www.ICGtesting.com
Printed in the USA
LVHW022007260819
629003LV00002B/2